Will the Vikings
Ever Win
the Super Bowl?

Also by Jim Klobuchar

How to Survive Pro-Football Sunday

True Hearts and Purple Heads

Tarkenton *(with Fran Tarkenton)*

SuperBowl

1	67	Packers KanCity
2	68	Packers Oakland
3	69	Jets Baltimore
4	70	KansasCity Vikings
5	71	Baltimore Dallas
6	72	Dallas Miami
7	73	Miami - Washington
8	74	Miami Vikings
9	75	Pittsburg - Vikings
10	76	Pittsburg - Dallas
11	77	Oakland - Vikings
12	78	Denver - Dallas

Will the Vikings Ever Win the Super Bowl?

by Jim Klobuchar
with Jeff Siemon's Journal

HARPER & ROW, PUBLISHERS

NEW YORK, HAGERSTOWN, SAN FRANCISCO
LONDON

A section of photographs follows page 118.

Portions of this work originally appeared in The Minneapolis Star-Tribune.

FIRST EDITION

Designed by Sidney Feinberg

Library of Congress Cataloging in Publication Data

Klobuchar, Jim.
  Will the Vikings ever win the Super Bowl?
  1. Minnesota Vikings (Football team)
I. Siemon, Jeff, joint author. II. Title.
GV956.M5K59 1977   796.33′264′09776579   77–3755
ISBN 0–06–012411–3

77 78 79 80 10 9 8 7 6 5 4 3 2 1

Preface

In the country's present arrangement of values, to win the Super Bowl is to land on Venus and part the Red Sea in the same three hours on prime time.

For the winner it is both a space odyssey and a consecration. If you do it you earn the public's permanent genuflection. Nothing you do afterward can diminish you or revoke your immortality.

Losing the Super Bowl, on the other hand, consigns the luckless wretch to the category of the George McGoverns, the bad angels and the downtown Burbanks. You are a balloon for the comedian or an outcast of proper society.

That is, if you lose one Super Bowl.

If you lose two Super Bowls, you are considered a suitable candidate for the nation's psychiatric couch and suspected of a course of conduct hazardous to public order.

If you lose three Super Bowls, you are expunged from polite conversation and accorded the same fate as the village wartcarrier.

There is no clearly classified disgrace for a team that loses the

Super Bowl four times. Nobody could possibly lose the Super Bowl four times in four attempts.

The Minnesota Vikings have lost the Super Bowl four times in four attempts.

Scholars have attempted to explain it; $5 bettors from Duluth have deplored it. The Vikings have been accused of being under-motivated and over-quarterbacked. They are said to be too old and too light. Arrayed against either the American Football Conference champion or Disney's halftime entertainment, they are charged with being out of their class.

In Minnesota last January, the Vikings' loss to Oakland in Super Bowl XI provoked a mass depression unmatched since the last closing of the walleye season.

None of the accusations lodged against the Minnesota Vikings in the wake of their Super Bowl defeats is heard very often or very seriously during the other twenty weeks of the season. For ten years it has been one of the most successful athletic organizations in the world. Yet because it has not won the Super Bowl it now has a credibility comparable to the man who cried wolf.

In this book we do pay obligatory service to some of the theories and remedies. Among them you will find a remarkable one that would require a wholesale overhaul of the Vikings' hygienic patterns.

What Jeff Siemon and I want to do mostly, though, is to take a reflective look at an unusual football team in an unusual season, 1976, when, in the cool and uncluttered lexicon of Bud Grant, "we shot sevens on the dice all season and then in Pasadena came up craps."

That the Minnesota Vikings have made this an operational routine for the past eight years has aroused both the scorn and bafflement of the critics and the dismay of their multitudes on the prairie. They probably deserve little of this. But as Grant again correctly observes, it is not something for a Super Bowl loser to cry about. More than any other game in America, but more particularly in the fan reaction to it, the Super Bowl is the Roman Colosseum of big-time athletics. There is no room for temporizing, no restraint in the glorification of the winner and no consolation for the loser. The winner gets the hand of the Emperor's lady. The loser is chopped meat.

But how about the people who have played for this four-time loser in the Super Bowl? And what of their 1976 year of deliverance itself? Grandly destined by all appearances, it ended in a Don Quixote crusade gone amuck. The knight's battleaxes were helplessly imbedded in the Oakland windmill and the horse galloped riderless back to Costa Mesa.

Some of these people are funny and a few irritating. Many of them are continually fascinating, no matter what happened the second week in January. And maybe that's what gives an edge to their profile in the eyes of the journalist who has watched them for years—Tarkenton, Page, Eller, Marshall, Hilgenberg, Foreman and the rest. So fruitful in the fall, so barren in January.

Among this group, of course, you should include Jeff Siemon. He is a linebacker, an all-pro, and a practicing Christian. The latter is not said gratuitously. His faith is a crucial part of Jeff Siemon's football, focusing it, enlarging it at times, limiting it at others. He is a witness in this book to the day-to-day slapstick, the triumphs and drudgeries and defeats, the delights and annoyances that constitute a football team's regimen from August to January. His journal serves as a framework for our chronicle of an uncommon year in the life of a football team. He has been part of it for five years, and he looks at the team's ambitions and struggles with the unsentimental candor—but no lack of warmth— which is characteristic of Jeff Siemon.

Braided with Siemon's impressions are those of the journalist-witness, who sometimes sees the game and the athletes a little differently. But he is no less amazed that anybody in Faribault, Minnesota, would want to lynch a guy like Tarkenton on the night of January 9, 1977.

They could at least have waited until they looked at the film.

JIM KLOBUCHAR

April 1977

Will the Vikings
Ever Win
the Super Bowl?

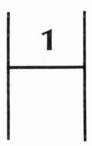

An hour after the Minnesota Vikings lost their fourth Super Bowl game in eight years the telephone rang in the home of a suburban Minneapolis housewife.

The woman greeted her husband, a brash and effusive young attorney whose voice came to her draped in disoriented chords of melancholy. She had been expecting him for hours; he was wanted to help supervise their four-year-old, who had been honking around the house with a bad cough and an untuned kazoo. Now the husband's explanations were barely comprehensible. His voice was spent, his spirit ravaged. He had been watching the Super Bowl game, he explained.

The telephone line bristled with silence.

The attorney awaited condolences, his eyes closed to receive the comfort of his beloved. None came. She didn't follow football. It was a dereliction that had stirred gossip for years in their neighborhood. She didn't even know who had won.

"Come home," she instructed him icily. "We need groceries."

He arrived thirty minutes later, without groceries and without the vaguest acknowledgement that he was again in the presence of hearth and family. Mutely he walked to his room and packed his bags. Emerging, he swept out of the house, drove to a bar a few blocks away, belted three drinks and returned home—where in five minutes he had confronted his wife with a notice of separation. It was couched in flawless legal language that included liberal visitation rights. He then disappeared once more into his room.

The wife flung the document into the fireplace and completed the evening gnawing pensively on one of the two large steaks she had prepared during her husband's flight to the saloon.

The next morning he left for work, and he returned at the usual hour without a syllable of apology or explanation.

Variations of this melodrama probably occurred in scores of Minnesota communities the night of January 9, 1977. Psychologists are positive of it. The rest of the civilized world reacted to another Viking defeat in the Super Bowl with the same general attitude of Perry Mason fans viewing his latest courtroom battle with Hamilton Burger. What made it fascinating was the pure inevitability of it. There was never much question who was going to lose; the suspense lay in how it would be accomplished this time.

Over the years the Viking performances in the Super Bowl have built up in the nation's television galleries a thick layer of jaded condescension and bemusement. It entitles them to a mocking sense of superiority when the network squads of football analysts appear before each Super Bowl game to direct their breezy erudition at the thrills that lie ahead for the viewers and sponsors this afternoon. It is going to be so gripping the Goodyear blimp is shuddering in expectation. Lookathere, man, at that big ole blimp about to shudder. Camera pans to Goodyear blimp, which does its best to shimmy in order to reinforce Don Meredith, who often requires much reinforcement on Sunday afternoon.

The affirmation of the American idyll once took the form of driving into the country on Sunday afternoon. Then it became building a home. Values change as progress asserts itself. The person who takes a drive in the country today is courting bankruptcy. He who builds a house may be courting commitment. So to establish membership in the great society today, one watches the Super Bowl. Like most carefully choreographed extravaganzas it has gone beyond mere entertainment for the watcher and has become a duty. Watching the Super Bowl has become a subliminal phrase in the Pledge of Allegiance.

America is watching every Super Bowl Sunday, all right, but in the Super Bowls involving the Vikings it has shed any illusion that the Super Bowl may be a contest. If you doubt that, play the word-association game with the television watcher in Woonsocket, South Dakota. Give him the words Vikings and Super Bowl. Ask him to summon an image. (No sexism is intended; you can also ask her.) You will get a clear consensus quickly. The Minnesota Vikings will play each Super Bowl exactly as they did the last. They will play earnestly, ineptly and with a discernible aura of doom, like a man walking under a falling redwood. They play so predictably they have inspired among football touts a system of handicapping similar to racetrack form sheets. In the Super Bowl the Vikings can be expected to fumble on their opponent's 1-yard line at least once, throw to the wrong people, fall hopelessly behind after 30 minutes and score a consolation touchdown. And Alan Page will leave the bench 10 or 15 seconds before the end of the game —and be surprised that everybody didn't do it.

On January 9 the scorn visited on their champions from Nome to Diamond Head to Flushing Meadow plunged fans of the Minnesota Vikings—especially those living in Minnesota— into demoralization and bitterness with few parallels in the chronicles of mass despair. In Minnesota, years of denial in the Super Bowl have invested the public with the same kind of red-eyed solidarity forged by the defenders of the Alamo. It has made the Minnesota football congregations and their yearnings the target of a menagerie of pop psychologists. Visitors to Minneapolis and St. Paul and its enclaves often are startled when exposed to the population's fixation with the Vikings. It has a character different from the conventional frenzies elsewhere, and what makes it unique in Minnesota is the cross of the Super Bowl. Both the football team and its followers spend much of their lives in postures of atonement—an attitude that's hard to handle because the team annually wins 70 percent of its games and usually clinches the Central Division title by Columbus Day. To be a true social virtue, football hysteria has to be utterly free and unreasonable. In Minnesota no such to-hell-with-tomorrow jubilation is permitted.

They may howl on Sunday afternoon and get swacked in the parking lot ice fields and toast each other with upraised brat-wurst, but when they get home and finish the television replays on the ten o'clock news, the last question they ask before turning the knob is: "They can't possibly screw up the Super Bowl this year, can they?"

History records that they can. And yet what happens on the frozen plains of Metropolitan Stadium and on the television screen each Sunday dominates the cultural life of Minnesota to a degree that baffles most social scientists. This, after all, is a land of political and social achievement and innovation. It is a progressive and civil place. It has world-famous hospitals and schools, prosperous farms, lovely lakes and woods and practically no social strife. The most lurid political corruption of the past three years was the legislature's decision to increase its per diem expense allowance. The state has given the world Charles Lindbergh, Hubert Humphrey, Walter Mondale, Judy Garland, Marlon Brando, Hiawatha, Eugene McCarthy and Snoopy. But for three years the most popular figure on Minnesota television was a second-string defensive end, Bob Lurtsema. His lumpily honest face and laryngitic voice made him the alter ego of hundreds of thousands of people who were ecstatic about the idea of the people's benchwarmer peddling passbooks for a savings and loan house.

When the Vikings traded him in the fall of 1976, thousands sent or telephoned sympathy messages. But if the social scientists couldn't understand that, the psychologists did. It's true

4

that Minnesota was a relatively sophisticated environment, they agreed, but practically nothing happened in Minnesota to generate rage, bliss or even, in some weeks, measureable interest. A bank almost never got held up. There were no riots, unless you counted the annual All-Serbs Day Picnic in Chisholm on the Iron Range. November newlyweds were known to spend their honeymoons at a remote lakeside cottage on Lake Winnibogshish, watching the ice form. Such long sieges of serenity may be good for heaven but are bad for a healthy psyche, the scholars agree. Thus, when professional football and a winning team arrived, the search for a serviceable convulsion pretty well ended.

It would be climaxed in that epic hour when Commissioner Pete Rozelle would stand flushed and benign as he always does and, trying not to reveal that Tom Brookshier has just stepped on his toe, present the Super Bowl trophy to the Minnesota Vikings.

Such an hour might have occurred in New Orleans in January 1970, in Houston in January 1974 and/or in New Orleans in January 1975. It didn't. The Vikings were confused by Kansas City in Super Bowl IV, crunched by Miami in Super Bowl VIII and slowly smothered by Pittsburgh in Super Bowl IX. Their popularity never waned much among their fans, but their credibility around the country was shot.

The Vikings couldn't win the big one. Neither could Francis Tarkenton. When you came down to it, neither could Charlie Goodrum, a relatively innocent offensive lineman. By rights he had to suffer the collective guilt with all the others. Fred Cox couldn't kick the big one and Bud Grant couldn't coach it. Even the trainer, Fred Zamberletti, was suspect. He couldn't tape the big one. These accusations were hotly challenged by the fans in public; but the fans shared the suspicions in private, and they anguished over them.

They did so partly because this was a football team that won with profound regularity. It was widely reputed to have character, respect for authority and the flag and an unmatched ability to stand at attention for the national anthem in sunlight and in blizzard. The Vikings were the good knights of professional football. The Lions were squabblers, the Dolphins were bellyachers and the Raiders operated some kind of training school for incorrigibles and a roost for odd ducks; the Vikings were orderly and true.

Justice almost certainly would decree that the Minnesota Vikings of all teams should be granted one vision—and therefore at least one year's possession of the chalice Pete Rozelle carried with him to each Super Bowl Sunday.

The season of 1976, it was decided, would yield that vision. The decision was unanimously made by the Minnesota Vikings and their loyalists. It was the kind of year the honorable old heads—belonging to such as Tarkenton, Jim Marshall, Carl Eller, Paul Krause, Alan Page, Fred Cox, Mick Tingelhoff and Wally Hilgenberg—could dedicate with one sustained and passionate reach for the prize of prizes. In this they were encouraged by the NFL schedule, which paired the Vikings against such non-terrorist organizations as the Seattle Seahawks, Philadelphia Eagles, New York Giants, Green Bay Packers and New Orleans Saints. They were also goaded by the possibility that if they missed in January 1977, some of them might not be back with Minnesota to try again in 1978; and most of them might therefore have seen their last of the Super Bowl. They received by far their most inspired encouragement, however, from the fans—to whom the thought of a fourth Super Bowl defeat was too mortifying to consider seriously.

And so the ship of hope sailed resolutely into Pasadena in January 1977. The world, or that portion of it represented by the Los Angeles dailies, smiled omnisciently. Jim Murray of the Los Angeles *Times* couldn't understand why they let the Vikings have visas. They shouldn't be allowed into California for fear of contaminating the Los Angeles Rams, who were still undefeated in the Super Bowl on the basis of no appearances in eleven years. Jim was unlike his confederates in the Los Angeles press, whose distaste for the Vikings was an expression of the elderly beachboy's suspicion of normalcy. Murray's bile flowed from deeper wells: He had been trapped two weeks before in the women's john of Metropolitan Stadium in Minnesota.

This might not have been a traumatic adventure if it had occurred in the Los Angeles Coliseum, where Murray almost certainly would have blundered into at least one other member of the L.A. press corps in the same parlor to share his travail. At the Met, however, he was victimized by the medieval social attitudes in Minnesota, where women's johns are generally reserved for women. Murray's post-game urgencies were so fierce that he was forced to seek sanctuary well short of the men's room and burst into the other, which was unoccupied at the time. He was devastated a few minutes later to discover the doors had been locked from the outside. The thought of the Los Angeles *Times* publishing without his usual compassion and civility stirred Murray to preternatural strength. Ultimately he pried open a door, barely escaping arrest by convincing a cop he was a Viking tailgater. Murray assumed this was the only explanation acceptable for deranged behavior in Minnesota.

The experience may have changed Jim Murray for life, depriving him of the restraint and tenderness that usually characterize his work. As a result the Vikings were welcomed on their arrival in California in Super Bowl week by a Murray column that appealed to the Geneva Convention to create new football rules by which an instant slaughter of the Minnesota Vikings could be avoided or at least delayed.

Murray proposed that Commissioner Pete Rozelle, acting on behalf of the Red Cross, limit Oakland to four points for each touchdown. It should also be forced to kick off after all scores, Viking or Raider, play with ten men in the second half, require Kenny Stabler to pass right-handed, tie Cliff Branch in a potato sack and spot Minnesota 14 points going into the game.

Murray's theses naturally aroused snarls of loathing among the arriving purpleheads. In retrospect, though, it should be recorded that none of the proposed rules would have saved

Minnesota, not even the 14-point handicap.

The derision directed against the Vikings in California that week was broadly based. It extended to the gambling sharks in Nevada, the alleged gambling guru from CBS, Jimmy the Greek Snyder, and evidently to the California weatherman. He served a snowstorm four days before the game to stall Mrs. Bud Grant and her young on their way over one of the California passes in a camper trailer.

The Vikings' subsequent 32–14 defeat vindicated all of the braying contempt that preceded them. It led the *Times'* Bob Oates to demand in print the next day that the Vikings be legally barred from ever appearing in another Super Bowl game. In Oates' account this ultimatum took precedence over the score, a detail Bob sometimes considers an obstacle in presenting his wisdom to the public.

Within hours the Minnesota Vikings became a kind of national comedy relief. The Vikings had surpassed William Jennings Bryan in fiascos and were closing in on Mussolini's army. Nail down everything that moved on the dinner table, the comics giggled, because if you didn't the Vikings were almost certain to fumble it or throw it for an interception.

In Minnesota the ignominy was total and unrelieved. For days the natives moved about in robotlike attitudes, trudging through an emotional no-man's-land, impervious even to the barbs and raillery from Los Angeles.

Eventually, however, the first symptoms of consciousness returned, and with them came Theories, always sure evidence that the football fan is on the road to rehabilitation.

Theories swarmed and collided in the letters columns of the newspapers, in barber chairs, under hair dryers, in sausage factories and in the confessional. Rarely in the field of human endeavor have theories been advanced by so many to give so much illumination to a game which needed so little.

A thoughtful gravel pit worker from LeSueur, Minnesota, Andrew Anderson, theorized that the Vikings fail so miserably in the Super Bowl because of the unnatural behavior of their cholesterol. He explained to a reporter that he had volunteered for cholesterol studies at the University of Minnesota and was told by researchers that the Vikings probably were casualties of a form of spring fever when they played in warm weather cities in January.

"Because of our hard winters," he wrote, "we build up more fat than people do in warmer parts of the country. Toward springtime this fat begins to dissipate and our blood thins. There is a period when the chemical changes bring about a light-headedness and a muscular sluggishness. We generally call this spring fever. Now if you suddenly are transferred to a warm climate in the middle of winter, the same phenomenon occurs. It's one thing to get spring fever if it's spring and you're 19 years old looking for romance. It's another thing if you're in Pasadena chasing Fred Biletnikoff."

This proposition, while interesting, might have raised more questions than it solved—at least one of them by Biletnikoff himself.

Mrs. Glorine Dancik of northeast Minneapolis blamed herself.

"I really believe they were sabotaged by my own pre-game plan, which consisted of a clean house, meals prepared in advance, three kids down for naps by 2 P.M. so momma could put her feet up and watch the entire game without interruption. It was completely selfish of me. While I watched the game in comfort, the purple gang destroyed themselves in front of God and everyone. On every Sunday when I had to spend the whole afternoon charging around the house cleaning up and preventing the kids from catching awful diseases, the Vikings won. If I saw them even for a quarter, they lost. On Super Sunday I saw the whole game. They got hammered. If I stayed around for the post-game interviews their bus back to the hotel would have gone over a cliff."

Millie Payne of southeast Minneapolis speculated that Alan Page's hemorrhoids had doomed the Vikings. Dennis Kinnamon insisted that the day before the game, Grant should have shifted Carl Eller, Doug Sutherland and Matt Blair from the left side of the Vikings' defense—where they had played every play for years and years—to the right side and flop Jim Marshall, Wally Hilgenberg and Page from the right side—where they had played every play for years.

"Wouldn't it have boggled Oakland's minds," he asked, "to prepare yourself all week to face Marshall and line up against Eller?"

It almost certainly would have accomplished one breakthrough, a Viking coaching assistant later conceded. "Everybody on the field on both sides would have been disoriented, and nobody would have lined up onside."

The most popular theory centered on the so-called runnerup syndrome that has supposedly blighted Minnesota's struggle to excel in the political, athletic and even the erotic arenas. It was a theory first propounded by a newspaper editorialist in, of all places, Buffalo, New York, a community reputed to be one of the lost battalions among America's civic legions. Minnesota, the writer suggested, had a gift approaching genius for finishing second. He cited Hubert Humphrey as vice president and later finishing second to Richard Nixon; the Minnesota Twins finishing second to the Los Angeles Dodgers in their only World Series; the Minnesota Vikings finishing second in every Super Bowl they played. The theory snowballed after January 9, 1977, with fresh evidence from Pasadena and from Washington, D.C., where Walter Mondale was preparing to assume the second highest office in the land.

Every Minnesota boy (and girl) now grew up aspiring to be lieutenant governor, it was suggested. Further research turned up a revelation that in all of the well-documented history of amour, there had never been a world-famous lover from Minnesota. It was said to be a measure of Minnesota's futility in this field that one of its most prominent candidates, the Indian princess Winona, flung herself off a cliff into the Mississippi for reasons that were lost in the bubbles.

None of this conjecture disturbed a South Dakota professor,

John Milton. He saw in the Vikings' finishing second in the Super Bowl a serene acceptance of a role that may have been written in the stars. Someplace on earth there should be a land that has remained largely immune to the corruptive influences of success. Mr. Milton admitted it is a distinction not unanimously envied. "But isn't it possible," he asked, "that there is something in the Minnesota character that prevents those of us who are Minnesota natives from scratching, fighting, biting, committing mayhem and getting psyched up just to be called No. 1? Some of the Super Bowl winners, for instance, have been headquartered in cities that thrive on spectacle: Miami, Dallas, New York and Oakland."

Oakland, professor? Is that a direct quote?

The scholar would not be dissuaded.

"Furthermore, while Minnesota is cold in the winter it does not hold any national records that I know of, although it certainly would qualify for the playoffs there. It extends to civic virtues. While Minneapolis is a beautiful city, it's likely that San Francisco is more beautiful and New Orleans more exciting. And so on. I think we Minnesotans are subconsciously content to be *near* the top but not quite *at* the top. I believe this characteristic was transmitted by good Scandinavians without ego problems. I do not find it all bad. It may be a healthy sign of sanity combined with talents that are substantial even though they set no records. We do our work without a compulsion to be spectacular. In the long run we probably accomplish more, not burning out easily."

With this theory the professor revealed himself to have the triple threats of bravery, modesty and astigmatism. It was modest for the professor to assert a belief that best is not bliss; it was brave of him to claim Minnesota is not the coldest place on earth in winter (something the Los Angeles Rams could disprove instantly); and there may be something wrong with his eyes that he detects no militant egos. You could not have lived in Minnesota for any length of time and ignored such people as Jeno Paulucci, Robert E. Short, a part-time resident named

11

Billy Martin, and the Steelworkers local in Duluth, all of whom at one time or other have shown an ardent faith in biting and scratching as proper qualities in a fight.

Beyond this, the old University of Minnesota coach, Bernie Bierman, was part Scandinavian. Bierman usually left bliss and tranquility to Northwestern. On Mondays after the rare weekends when he didn't win, Bierman gave everybody 15 laps around the field. If his relatives were visiting he ran them, too.

The other problem with Milton's theory is that only a handful of the Vikings are native Minnesotans. Maybe Andrew Anderson's cholesterol theory made more sense.

While the fans were groping about in this state of bewilderment, Alan Page returned home from California two days after the Super Bowl. Innocently he granted an interview. Yes, he was disappointed that the Vikings lost the Super Bowl, he said, but the march of mankind would not halt abruptly because of it. In the life of Alan Page, he said, playing in the Super Bowl or winning it did not constitute a day of transformation, although he played as hard as he was capable of playing. He understood the fans' emotional involvement in the game, he said, and that was good. He asked, "Was there any way that this game really had a critical impact on the life of the country or the lives of the people who played in it and watched it? There was no way winning or losing the Super Bowl is going to change my life. And if it changes the life of anybody else, I feel sorry for them. If the price of oil goes up 10 percent, that has impact. It means something for a lot of people, in dollars and cents, where you go and where you eat. Right after the Super Bowl a lot of people were ecstatic and a lot of them were depressed, but how much difference did it really make in their lives?"

Leaving the bench 15 seconds before the end of the game, Page explained, represented no symbolic act by Alan Page, no statement of principle. "All it meant," he said, "was that the season was over. We were still trying to score a touchdown in the last minute of the game, and I'm not sure why. Yes, it meant some consolation points. I don't know why we needed them. We couldn't win. The game was over."

To help fans find a solution to the mystery of the Vikings' performances in the Super Bowls, Page offered a revolutionary thought: At least on the days they played, he said, it was quite possible that Kansas City, Miami, Pittsburgh and Oakland were better than the Vikings.

It was a stunning idea. Few people in Minnesota had seriously considered this theory—which, after all, seemed very thin in cholesterol. Instead, the part of the Viking public that had recovered enough to talk denounced Page's remarks about hyperinvolvement. They reacted as though he had trampled on their birth certificates.

The episode confirmed Page's instinctive wariness about being frank with fans and newspapers. Newspapers, after all, cannot put shadings of meanings in the limited count of a four-column, 48-point headline. Alan Page was never uproariously popular with the public, mostly because of his refusal to adopt a moist eye and abject lip when losing was supposed to dictate that. He now became a lightning rod for the natives' chagrin and aggression.

"I've got a brother-in-law who can't sleep the week before the Super Bowl," seethed Eugene Johnson, a fan, "a brother who can't sit through a whole Viking game in fear of a coronary, a sister who burns a purple candle during Viking games and a number of friends who suffer from a whole assortment of maladies during the Viking season. Sure we're involved, and what the hell is wrong with that? Some of the most vocal players have lost it, the pride of winning. Football has become so mechanical to them that all feeling is lost. Sure they want to win, but only because it is the thing to do, besides fattening their already oversized pay envelopes. It seems many of them could care less. Why should they? Most don't live here anyway. They can go home and forget it until next season.

"The over-involved fans, on the other hand, are left here to

13

freeze their fannies for three more frosted months trying to figure out what in the hell happened in the Super Bowl. Sure we are upset. Just when these people have us convinced they can conquer all worlds by beating all possible rivals in their so-familiar 'dump the ball off the halfback' fashion, they fall flat on their butts in the Super Bowl and, worse yet, with only a half-hearted effort. Is this by chance the ultimate of all Bud Grant practical jokes? That thought has occurred to me. After all, he's done it to us four times now."

This recital qualified Eugene Johnson for the kitchen-sink award in all-systems hostility. It was an encyclopedia of theories, fully annotated and indexed, spreading blame evenly among complacent Vikings, greedy Vikings, ungrateful Vikings, alien Vikings and that posturing slapstick comedian of the sidelines, Harry Peter Grant.

"I never said the fan shouldn't be involved," explained a dazed Alan Page a couple of days later. "I just asked about degrees of involvement and priorities."

So it came down to nuances of language.

But don't ever again mess with nuances, Page, three days after losing 32–14 in the Super Bowl, when frost is already beginning to form on four million fannies. This might not be totally accurate meteorologically—but what a slogan for the Vikings to carry into their next Super Bowl game!

The prospect of the Minnesota Vikings playing in another Super Bowl, as early as 1978 in fact, is one to send unmanageable shakes through network executives, sponsors and perhaps the National Football League itself. Oates in Los Angeles candidly questions the constitutionality of allowing the Vikings to play in this game at all.

Yet they are likely to be back within a matter of a few years. The presence of Grant alone almost insures it. Practically nobody coaches better in professional football, and almost nobody wins as much from September to December. In addition, the Vikings play in the Central Division of the NFL. For many years the Central Division, Minnesota excepted, could not have achieved parity with Hogan's Heroes let alone the other divisions of the NFL. It has improved stoutly in the last couple of years, but it was still less than paralyzing as an aggressor force in the NFL in 1976. And, once safely past their Central Division rivals, the Vikings stand a fair chance of playing in undomed Metropolitan Stadium in December in their playoff games. In the minds of people like Jack Youngblood of the Los Angeles Rams, this alone is grounds for deporting the state of Minnesota to Iceland. Either Iceland, as he observed through clanking teeth and trembling blue lips in the Rams' locker room last December, "or wherever the Eskimos live, because that's where this game should have been played."

There is one other consideration.

The Minnesota Vikings have been, for ten years, one of the superb football teams in the land. If they have not won the Big One, the one which would exonerate them in the minds of millions who are devoted to the jock mythology, they have won scores of uncapitalized big ones. Each of these, at the time, offered its own valid measurement of the football team's quality. The Vikings have kicked a lot of butts and have beaten a lot of football teams called great; and they have won year in and year out with a kind of presence and professional dignity that is sometimes mistaken for—and derided as—cold, gray mechanicalism.

The image is a joke.

The football team has personalities that run the spectrum of the bizarre, the attractive, the straight and the harrowing, and they are worth examination. That is what follows, in the framework of Jeff Siemon's journal of the 1976 season and the reflections of a journalist who has watched the Vikings for years, not always with full comprehension. The Vikings have entertained millions for years and most recently acted as the supporting cast for the Super Bowl card show, and they may very well be back in another Super Bowl shortly.

And is everybody truly ready for that?

Is anybody?

2

From Jeff Siemon's journal

Wednesday, September 8, 1976   The talk in the dressing room today was about the coming arrival of Ahmad Rashad (formerly Bobby Moore) in a Viking uniform. We acquired him in a trade this week. Football players are some of the world's most accomplished gossips. I've heard everything from fears about Ahmad's alleged bad attitude to talk about some incident that gave him a reputation of being a troublemaker of sorts. I've heard rumors that he tends to be lazy and that Jack Patera at Seattle traded him because of his suspect knee and contempt for practice. That's the sort of stuff that bounces off the walls in a pro football locker room. The players don't necessarily buy it. They just exchange it. I've also heard tremendous hopes and expectations about how Ahmad Rashad can fit in on this team and become the deep receiver many of us think we need. I have been satisfied with Sammy White, and Jim Lash has always been consistent. I'm not certain Ahmad will ever start as a Minnesota Viking, but ought to be interesting. I think winning football brings out the best in people. We may have potential problems on this team, despite its reputation for order and discipline. These might surface if

16

we lost a string of football games. But I think also we have the kind of competitive environment to bring out the best in Rashad. I played against him four years when I was at Stanford and he was at Oregon. He was a running back there. He was a great college football player, and I know he has huge potential as a receiver. The Vikings are his fourth team in the NFL. He ought to be ready.

Our small prayer group met again today, Robert Miller, Amos Martin, Wes Hamilton, Doug Kingsriter and myself. Doug was cut by the Vikings a few days ago after three years in the NFL, and is experiencing the difficult period all players feel at a time like this. We have committed ourselves to meet once a week throughout the season and pray specifically for one another and for the team collectively. Our wish is that through an outpouring of God's spirit, a unique unity and fellowship might be developed among our teammates. Our special prayer is that those who do know Christ, but have chosen to disregard him, might come to a deeper relationship with him, one that creates in them a desire to put him first in everything they do.

Thursday, September 9   We got our first look today at Ahmad Rashad. It's evident he is a great athlete, and if his knee is sound he's going to help us. He didn't make any special plays in practice; he didn't make many catches. Just watching him run his patterns you can tell he is a player of rare ability, timing and gracefulness. I had to laugh getting reacquainted with him. I knew him as Bobby Moore and it's hard to remember to call him Ahmad. I'm much interested in talking to him about his orthodox Muslim faith. I've done some study on comparative religions over the past few years and am interested to see how a practicing Muslim supports the tenets of his faith.

Carl Eller was back at practice today, recovering from his broken thumb. He won't be able to play in our opener at New Orleans Sunday. I think Mark Mullaney, who will start in place of Moose, is going to be a first-rate football player, but to be perfectly honest I'd have to say I'm worried about how Mark will perform right now starting his second season. New Orleans is sure to try to exploit his

17

inexperience, and I'm hoping he gives us the kind of game to match his potential.

Friday, September 10 Jocko Nelson, the linebacker coach, handed out our special team sheets today and got some laughs. They told Jocko it must be some kind of mistake because Roy Winston was listed as a starter on the punt team. The fan would not consider this especially hilarious, but it broke up some of Winston's teammates. Winston is in his fifteenth season of pro football. He has been a starting linebacker since 1963 and he is one of the good, honorable men of the National Football League. But reputations don't mean much when they get out their harpoons in the locker room. Moony isn't starting this year, and it may be his last in pro ball. It's been ten years since he played on one of the kicking teams, which are usually reserved for the younger or specialty players. If it bothered Roy he didn't make any announcement about his feelings. As a matter of fact he laughed about it in a comment he made to me. "You come into the league on the special teams," he said, "and you go out the same way." I felt some sadness about that. I've always admired and appreciated Roy as much as anyone on the team and I knew he would work as hard on the punting teams as he ever did as a linebacker.

I talked to Francis Tarkenton today about Ahmad's injury. I said Fred Zamberletti, the trainer, was wary about Rashad's knee. Francis shrugged it off. He said there was no big problem. I admitted my own knee injury when I came into the league seemed worse than Rashad's. But I said it was different for a receiver playing with a bad knee because he needs all of his speed and movement. Tarkenton said he knew about all that but after watching Rashad the first day he would let other people worry; he had no worries of his own. He told me he had seen Rashad just one day and couldn't remember another receiver with better hands or better moves. Tarkenton is the quarterback. That pretty well closed the case.

Sunday, September 12 We hammered the Saints, 40–9. New Orleans started the game fumbling and bungling and never stopped. Before they knew what was happening we had them 13–0 and they

18

played the rest of the game in shell shock. I almost felt sorry for Hank Stram, the New Orleans coach, although one guy who definitely did not feel sorry for Stram was Bud Grant.

I'm sure Grant has never forgiven Stram for the remarks he made during and after the 1970 Super Bowl game between the Vikings and the Kansas City Chiefs, which was Stram's team then. Stram let himself be wired for sound during the game, and the tapes were played back later. It wasn't really offensive stuff, but Stram did say "lookit them running around like a Chinese fire drill," and "it's just like stealing," and things like that. He got fired in Kansas City, and we may have had some small role in that because we blasted them on the last game of the 1974 season, and they really looked bad. I know Stram thinks he can turn the New Orleans situation around, and maybe he can, but he got off to a terrible beginning against us.

I really wasn't quite ready for the Bud Grant halftime speech. It was in character for Grant to say some of the things he did, that although the score was 30–3 it was no time to be letting up but to keep the kind of killer instinct that good teams need to turn a 30–3 rout into something even more positive. At the end of his halftime remarks, Bud said something like, "let's pour it on these guys because I want to be able to say at the end of the game it was just like stealing." There were howls in the dressing room over that. But I was almost floored flying back after the game to learn that Bud actually said it in his opening remarks in the post-game press conference. He might have done it half in comedy and half on the square. When he deadpans you the way he does you're never sure. I do know Stram's coaching style, his flamboyance, and his airs about "the offense of the 1970s," have always offended Grant, although I think he does respect Stram's coaching ability.

Bud surprised me for this reason: He has often told his players it does no good to try to vent your bitterness on the other guy. He's told us a dozen times that getting involved with revenge distracts you and only hurts you and the team. I've always believed this was true in daily life as well as in the arena. It interested me that after all those years Bud still harbored feelings of revenge against Stram, although I'm sure he would never admit that publicly.

19

Obviously we didn't maintain our scoring pace of the first half, but a lot of our first half scoring was the result of New Orleans' mistakes, and we substituted pretty widely in the second half. Tarkenton and the offense had a romp. It was exciting to see the rookie, Sammy White, score his first pro touchdown in his native Louisiana, before all of his relatives in the Superdome. He was so exuberant I thought he would explode. He's a fine young man, spontaneous and willing, a good athlete, and I think he is a tremendous addition to this football team.

Tuesday, September 14 Bob Lurtsema left the Vikings today. It was a jolt to all who played with him, although I don't know many who were surprised. Bob was nearly cut as the extra defensive lineman when the roster was trimmed to 43 last week, and it develops now that he was part of the deal for Ahmad Rashad. You hate to see a guy like Lurts leave, although you know the realities of pro football and you brace for those things. He was the fellow who came to the Vikings five years ago, ostensibly to replace Jim Marshall at defensive end. He never did, of course, but inside of two years a love affair bloomed between the fans and Lurts. I've never really seen it equalled in my years in football.

Everybody in Minnesota is familiar with the story. A savings and loan house looked around for some likeable benchrider to put in a television commercial series as the good, willing, everyman sort of character, and Bob caught on immediately. He's a bright guy and a good journeyman football player, but he doesn't have a grain of pretension in him, and the fans saw that truth right off. He really was a regular guy, their guy. They mobbed him wherever he went. He had that kind of exposure. If anything, he was just as popular with the players, which is a really rare combination. He was always there with the offhand squelch, the funny but harmless line in the locker room, something to tell us we might be in a glamorous business but we were still kids playing a game. The times when he was at his best in the locker room were when we needed his special kind of roughhouse tonic to pull us out of the blahs. He was one of those guys who never wanted or needed a facade.

20

A lot of players, and I'm not excepting myself, at some time or other have pretended a hardened, callous attitude because that's supposed to be impressive. If you think about it, you outgrow it. I don't think Bob ever had much trouble with that. He's a caring sort of person, and he has never found playing pro football inconsistent with that quality. A lot of the appearances he made, the things he did for people, he was never paid for. He didn't do them for the sake of maintaining an image, I'm sure. Lurts is one of those guys who makes himself available if somebody else needs him.

Thursday, September 16 Maybe Rams week has something to do with the kind of flareup that big Ed White and Duck White got involved in today at practice. Or maybe Duck White figures he will have to play against Los Angeles Sunday. Duck is our high draft choice rookie on the defensive line. Lurtsema is gone now. Eller is still bothered by his broken thumb. Mark Mullaney, who did well against New Orleans, is ailing, too. So all of a sudden we're in trouble for defensive linemen. Duck put on a terrific pass rush. He consistently got to the quarterback by beating Ed and Ron Yary, who are two of the best pass blockers in football. Naturally Duck got a lot of support from the defensive players watching the action. Ed would go back into the offensive huddle just glaring at us, and you could see his pride had been damaged. On one play Ed moved from guard to tackle, as he often does in the workouts to get himself ready in case there are injuries at tackle. Duck slammed into him, slipped around him and touched the quarterback. The chorus rose again from the defensive people. Ed was seething. The only thing on earth he wanted at that moment was to stick it to Duck whatever way he could. Ballplayers are like that, and it doesn't matter if they're teammates. They collided on the next play, and Ed blocked well. Duck slipped and went down. Now Ed is one of the finest people and the most thoughtful guy you'd want to meet, but when the rookie went down he couldn't resist taking another shot at him while Duck was on the ground. It was a pretty amazing spectacle. He got boos for that, and I know he felt awful about it afterward, but sometimes it *is* a jungle.

Our offense knows it's facing one of the best defensive lines in the world in the Rams, but it isn't getting much encouragement from our own Alan Page. Alan delights in disorganizing our offense. On a lot of plays he's got the speed and moves to do it. He was really enjoying himself today. Once he just tore past the offensive guard and mock-sacked the quarterback, giggling and howling as he did. Jerry Burns, the offensive coordinator, almost split an artery. "It's a damned good thing we're not playing the Rams, today," he told the offense. Alan corrected him. "It's a good thing," he said, "you're not playing us today."

You get the impression Alan is not always the most popular guy in the world with the Viking offense. But maybe all of this is good. We're getting loose for the Rams game, which has to be one of the critical ones of the season for us. They've got a huge offensive line, great receivers in Ron Jessie and Harold Jackson and powerful runners like Lawrence McCutcheon, John Cappelletti and Jim Bertelsen. Cappelletti has taken over for Bertelsen. That surprises me. I think Bertelsen has been a great football player.

The way people—coaches and fans and players—evaluate ball players always fascinates me. I read today that one of the best football players I've ever seen is out for the year, and I'll bet a lot of people never heard of him. Jim Braxton, the Buffalo blocking back, got hurt in the Monday game against Miami and is finished for 1976 because of surgery. I'll predict right now Buffalo won't win a handful of games, no matter how soon O. J. Simpson gets ready. Braxton is the most devastating blocker coming out of the backfield that I've ever played against. Sometimes a good, solid running back can play all year and make one or two blocks that will send linebackers wheeling and flying flat. Braxton makes those blocks *every game,* sometimes three and four times a game—real crunching, lights-out blocks. I haven't learned anything in this game if I'm not right about Braxton's injury costing Buffalo a respectable season. He's that important to them.

Friday, September 17   They gave Nate Allen the trashcan treatment today. Nate is our new defensive back from San Francisco.

He's a bubbly, talkative, naive sort of a guy who's going to be popular with this team and also pretty valuable because he hustles and he hits. We were watching film when Buddy Ryan, the line coach, told Neill Armstrong, the defensive coordinator, that Nate wouldn't be in today. Right about then Marshall and Page and a few others burst in rolling this trashcan, from which two legs—two human legs—were sticking out. They had shoved Nate Allen into the can and must have used three or four rolls of tape to secure him upside down. There was no way the guy could get out. In that condition they wheeled him all the way down the locker room to the film room, which at Midway Stadium in St. Paul where we practice must be at least 300 yards.

I imagine if the Rams have some spies around here they would have to wonder what kind of outfit they're going to face Sunday at the Met. On days like this you're not totally sure of it yourself. But I like it. There's a point where the intensity for a big game can overwhelm a team before it ever gets on the field. I think Nate Allen will be the first to testify that we have no such fears Sunday.

Saturday, September 18 My parents arrived from San Francisco. I love them, but I have to worry about the omens. The first time they saw me play pro football Fred Cox's field goal attempt hit the upright on the last play of the game and we lost to St. Louis 19–17. The second time was against Detroit two years later. We had beaten the Lions thirteen straight games. My folks showed up and we lost. They came to both Super Bowl games I played in, and we didn't win either of those. A year ago they saw me play in Los Angeles. We lost. We haven't lost more than a dozen football games or so in the five years I've been in pro ball, but my parents have been present for half of them. If it happens again I'm going to ask them to boycott our games.

I'm relaxed and comfortable for the game, though. It's one of those where you know you're going to face a very tough examination, a game for the pros, and you welcome that when you know you're ready mentally and physically. I feel that. I think most of the team does. It will be a grinder. The Vikings and Rams do that to each other. I have less nervousness now in the pre-game. I used to be something of a basket case. Time has made the pressure more bearable. Maybe that's professionalism. But that won't mean it will hurt less when those monsters on the Rams' offensive front tee off.

Sunday, September 19 It'll be years before I forget the Vikings-Rams game of September 1976. We played 75 minutes, five quarters, if there is such a thing, and it ended 10–10. It was savage football, but it was beautiful in a way, if you can combine those qualities. I say beautiful because our defense faced one crisis after another, and it responded. I don't know how there can be another team in football physically as strong as the Rams. After the game Grant called us together and said that had never been so proud of a team in his twenty years of coaching. He said we could remember we stood up to the pressure.

In one situation an interference call put the Rams on our 1-yard line with four downs to get in. We huddled, and you could see the faces drop. I said a few things. The emotion of a goal-line stand is usually a cumulative, surging thing that feeds on the last play. I've always felt that in a goal-line defense if you stop the first play you've got a good fighting chance to stop the next three because you've sown some doubt and everybody on the defensive line is pumping adrenalin. I'm not the world's most inspiring orator or cheerleader. I wouldn't be believable if I tried to be, especially on that defensive team with great veterans like Page, Eller and Marshall who have seen it all. I just said we could stop them, that we had the people and we had done it to these guys before, and we could stop them again, and we were going to do it. And on the first play Lawrence McCutcheon fumbled the ball.

The game was filled with really wrenching plays like that. Brent McClanahan fumbled for us when the game looked ready to be sewed up. Still, with a couple of minutes to go in the overtime we seemed to have it locked. Francis had the offense driving, and we were going in. Even if they stopped us we were close enough for an easy field goal by Fred Cox. But Francis decided we could score a touchdown. So he threw, and he didn't see their linebacker, Rick Kay, and the guy intercepted on the goal line. It was an agonizing way to finish a game that we seemed destined to win under dramatic

24

conditions. In those situations you just cannot allow yourself to probe for scapegoats. Did the offense let the defense down, vice versa? It just doesn't do anybody any good trying to assess blame. A football team simply has to accept it and move on. After all, there were so many times when we were on the brink of losing the game, and we somehow manage to survive. Offensively we didn't play as well this game. But we all knew that the day was soon coming when the offense would have to compensate for a loose defensive game. It's just ruinous for a team to harbor hostile feelings within itself about who might have won the game by doing this or not doing that, especially in a game like the Los Angeles game, which I thought was one of the most memorable the Vikings have played in my five seasons of pro football.

It was a shock to me when the reporters wanted to know what happened to our defense. Can you believe that? We played our guts out, we stopped them on the goal line twice, Nate Allen blocked Tom Dempsey's field goal that would have won the game in the last minute of overtime—and they wanted to know what happened to our defense. We gave up 260 yards on the ground, somebody pointed out. Sure we did. In *five* quarters. This was a team that decided days ago, with Pat Haden starting his first game at quarter-back, that it was going to stay on the ground all afternoon. With guys like Rich Saul, Tom Mack and Doug France on the offensive line and McCutcheon and Cappelletti running, wouldn't you?

I was standing by my locker, more beat up and sore than I've ever been in my life, trying to savor something from what Grant said after the game. And they wanted to know what went wrong with our defense. I have always had cordial relations with newspapermen. Most of them who cover pro football regularly I've found to be reasonably perceptive and aware. But they must be like football teams. They have to have their slumps, too. What was wrong with our defense? Nothing. We played great defense, I thought, when we had to play great defense.

I looked over to the corner where Francis was talking to reporters. There's always a swarm there. I sympathize with Bob Berry and Bob Lee, who locker next to Tarkenton. If they had a ten-dollar bill for every time they got stepped on, they could retire from the game. Win or lose, great game or mediocre game, the crowd is always present. I tried to reconstruct Fran's thinking on that overtime pass that was intercepted. And I imagined that it was really a tremendous burden he was carrying. But he's an uncommonly resilient guy and he won't let himself reveal hurt, psychological or physical. I don't think there is another guy who wants to win more or has a higher stake in pro football today than Francis Tarkenton. It's not only because of his reputation, or the craving we all share to get back into the Super Bowl game and bury all those ghosts about not winning the Big One. He has more at stake because of those drives that seem to impell and keep his world constantly churning. I'm sure he would have loved nothing better than to bring the team in for a touchdown. I'm sure a field goal was the furthest thing from his mind when he called the pass play, which is an attitude anybody who plays this game will understand. There was only a minimal risk of interception in the play he called. But there it was. He followed his instincts and his will, the same way he has been doing for sixteen years, and this time his decision was hung out there for millions to second-guess. He is a man who has made things happen all his life. He has pursued success exuberantly and found it in almost everything he has done. Under the circumstances I doubt he would feel remorse, or that he should be expected to, because he threw for an interception on the goal line. But the failure to win when it was so close—that was the burden for this or any other quarterback in that situation, but particularly a quarterback with Tarkenton's urges. And he carried it well.

I just don't know when I've been more drained physically and emotionally, by any experience, as I was by the game with the Rams. I remember coming off the field. I was a complete mess from helmet to shoes, and where there wasn't dirt there was pain. There wasn't any part of the body where I didn't ache. I had a bruise on my right calf where I was kicked, and it was tightening up. At the end of the game I was racked in the knee, and it was swollen. I got kicked hard in the left shin earlier in the game, exactly where it was bruised in New Orleans. I sprained my right wrist, which was swollen twice the normal size. Both of my hands were swollen from fending blockers.

26

Defensive linemen and linebackers get that condition all the time. Your hands take a beating where you hit the opponent's face mask or shoulder pads or helmet. You wear pads to protect yourself from that (unless you're Alan Page, who is really extraordinary that way) but it doesn't guarantee you any freedom from welts and pain. I also sprained my left forefinger, and hyperextended my right arm.

Nobody summoned an ambulance. Why should they? There were a couple of dozen guys just like me in the Viking locker room and a couple of dozen more in the Rams' room down the corridor at the Met.

In that half-stupor I looked up from our linebackers' corner in the dressing room and saw Alan Page in about the same condition. He kind of crooked a little smile when our eyes met. Words were unnecessary. What Page's smile and tired eyes said was that we both had been through a punishing, emotionally grating football game and threw into it our last drop of energy. So did the Rams. And nobody won, after all that striving and exertion and blood.

There was a thread of humor in that. We both knew we had played hard and, under the conditions, well. I just said, "Alan, after all of that I guess I'm glad we got at least a tie." I think the entire team felt that, and I'd be surprised if the Rams didn't. You don't go out wanting to settle for ties, and you don't play that way, either. But you don't lie to yourself in the locker room afterwards. The ball player knows when the scoreboard is telling the truth. The scoreboard at the Met after five quarters was probably telling the truth.

Grant put it in perspective. He said he didn't like the tie and that he knew we didn't, but if we played with that kind of intensity the rest of the year it was going to be a big season for us.

If the game itself was unforgettable, I don't know how to classify what happened afterward. It was one of those rare post-game incidents involving players and spectators, violent in a way, but also hilarious in retrospect. If I had to guess in advance what Viking ballplayer would be in the center of it, I would guess Wally Hilgenberg. Wally is forever involved, with the ball game, with the officials, with the opposing team, with fans. He wears his emotions on his collar, he is sometimes a clown and sometimes a flaming avenger and a lot of the time he's around the ball park he wants to take somebody's head off.

The post-game exodus for me started with a pleasant conversation with Rob Scribner of the Rams, a friend of mine and a Christian. We chatted near the stadium gate about football, spiritual things and others. Then we parted and I got into our car. There was a huge traffic jam because of some bridge construction in the area. I was driving toward the parking lot's main exit when suddenly I saw Wally get out of his car, leaving his wife Mary and two elderly people who were also passengers. What happened next had to be pieced together at Midway Stadium the next day before it made any sense. Wally was driving behind a small bus occupied by a bunch of low-life characters, drunk, rowdy, the works. In the back of the bus there was a door, and one of the characters was urinating out of it, in front of Wally's car. The guy was laughing and pointing at Mary, and soon afterward another one of the rockheads did the same thing. Wally couldn't take any more of that. He got out of the car and walked over to the bus, which was barely creeping in the traffic. Hilgenberg yelled at these bums, and they yelled back.

I could have told them that was a mistake.

Hilgenberg went wild at something they said. He kicked the door open and punched one of them. They closed the door in a hurry, but it didn't do any good because Hilgenberg kicked it in again and punched another guy.

They had enough people in there that they were going to pull him in and take him on, apparently, but he yanked loose and went back to his car, which is about where I picked up the action. As Wally returned to his car, two guys came out of the bus and walked up to Wally, who was behind the wheel.

That was their second mistake.

The third was when they opened their mouths. Wally got out and grabbed one of the guys by the throat. He nailed him with at least five hard punches, and I mean they were very sincere, malicious punches of the kind to attract the guy's attention.

About that time the other guy ran up, and now it was 2 on 1. I figured Wally was in control of the first situation, and obviously needed no help. But when the other one ran up, I got out of the car and charged to the scene, which I reached in about a dead heat with Mick Tingelhoff, Autry Beaman and Nate Allen. Even Fred Zamberletti, the trainer, was ready to get in. Before we got there the second guy jumped up on Hilgenberg's back. Wally pulled him loose, turned him around and gave him a couple of shots. The guy was sort of reeling and caroming around, and stumbled straight into Tingelhoff, who couldn't resist clouting the guy himself. I'm glad the incident didn't turn into a 15-round brawl because my hand hurt so badly I couldn't have hit anybody. How Wally could was beyond me.

Somebody came over and pulled these guys back into the bus, and it was none too soon because at that stage the faces of both of them looked like seven miles of bad road.

All of this happened in full view of the Rams' bus, which was moving slowly toward the road to the airport. They must have been amazed that the Vikings had any energy left after a game like that. A few cheered. I don't know who they were cheering.

I remembered talking to Wally five minutes after the game. He said it was the most bruising game he had ever experienced in his 15 years of college and professional football. He said he didn't know how anybody could hurt more than he did.

I told him an hour later I knew at least two guys who hurt more.

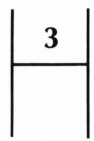

3

The wizards of television in their glass booths and sound trucks have been trying for years to depict the essence of the jocks-in-wonderland culture that so transfixes the American public on Sunday afternoon. It has been a struggle, but they could make it simple. If they want to mingle the allegories of pro football with its mud in the pits, they could document Jim Marshall.

With their multi-million-dollar camera gadgetry and the inescapable wisdom of the decommissioned quarterbacks in their broadcasting booths, the TV impresarios have grafted onto the American Sunday afternoon mentality a new kind of subconscious that would frighten Freud. It is filled with closeup images of tense warriors standing on the crater of crisis. It is good drama; the games themselves are superbly produced now. But they are so stuffed with dogma about the blinding complexity of pro football, and with stop-action stills freezing ferocity on the screen, no viewer can avoid gaping and shuddering.

But let's say they wanted one Sunday to portray professional football in all of its changes of mood and behavior. And they searched for a face, a name, a number, which in one two-and-a-half-hour time frame would allow them to unite the solemn and the kinky in pro football. And they would use this expressive face as a metaphor by which they could mix the game's poetry and pain. And let's say they also wanted to suggest that by living for the moment, this protagonist of theirs could achieve a certain kind of immortality—not so much by performance (eighteen years of pro football, while remarkably long, is not forever) but in the transcending joy the game gave to him and therefore to others.

And this undimmed excitement could override eighteen years of broken bones, pneumonia, attacks, fevers, linemen who outweighed him by 50 pounds, a humiliating run into the wrong end zone, tears, triumphs, financial fiascos, 250 parachute jumps, blizzards, post-game champagne parties and the simple pathology of the human body.

If you can play professional football in the teeth of all those distractions, is there any question you have achieved some kind of forever?

If there is room in professional football for all those colliding destinies, then professional football is more than a game. It is some kind of genie for today's America. It should have a face, and the face is Jim Marshall's.

It is mustached and rubbery. It is one of those faces where the forces of significance and tomfoolery seem to be at war. Slap a birdcage over it in practice and Jim Marshall's eyeballs roll and mug hugely. Midweek is playtime. The locker room is playtime. Howl and strut. The audience appreciates. Ball players. Who else? Is there anything on earth more restorative and merry than a football field in the middle of the fall, your name is Jim Marshall, everybody is crouching on the line of scrimmage, and some assistant coach is bitching and someplace on the stadium wall a bird is singing?

What's the big deal about a hereafter? Why not now?

But how many times has he cried, and vomited, and flinched because after nearly twenty years he got scared, too.

If Jim Marshall's football career and life were governed by the stars, as he believed on odd days (depending on his latest acquisition from psychic literature), then he must start his 225th consecutive pro football game in a game like the Vikings vs. Detroit on September 26.

It would be a pro record and the kind of football game with the inimitable Jim Marshall stamp. It would combine some good, gutbucket theater with harmless lunacy. In the post-mortems, in fact, there were some veteran Marshall aficionados who were willing to bet Jim Marshall was driving the team bus en route to the Lions' stadium in Pontiac. It arrived, after all, an hour late. The network executives were prostrate. The National Football League executives were demoralized. The Viking executives were in mud up to their knees directing traffic a mile from the stadium to speed the passage of the creeping bus. The game started 30 minutes behind schedule with the Vikings 15 yards in the hole because of the delay-of-game penalty. And Jim Marshall started his 225th straight football game.

The presence of Jim Marshall in all this disarray seemed, to calmer Jim Marshall watchers, to be perfectly normal.

If somebody else played his 225th consecutive game, the kickoff undoubtedly would have been executed at 1:06 P.M. or some drearily orthodox time close to it.

To a newspaperman in the pressbox, the juxtaposition of Marshall's 225th game with these wry events demanded a smile of recognition.

I had it right from the very beginning—16 years ago when Marshall played in the first game formally credited to the Minnesota Vikings. He was going to be a phenomenon. He had the heart of a Marco Polo and the fidgety bottom of a leprechaun. He wanted to fly, sail, climb, philosophize, evangelize, counsel, study and ride with the wind. On one weekend in the Beartooth Mountains years later, we did it together. It became the most tragic hour of both our lives, because a man died. We have since been bound by that shared grief, and always will be, although we have never socialized and at rare times—in moments of post-game misunderstanding—we have not especially liked each other.

32

The world's storehouse of natural phenomena, it occurred to me that Sunday in Detroit, is shrinking. Niagara is crumbling and Vesuvius is cooling. But here is Jim Marshall playing defensive end for the Minnesota Vikings, and one's momentary doubts about the permanence of the universe vanish. It is a kind of affirmation: Jim Marshall is in the Viking lineup; the sun is in the sky and the ocean spray is on the wind.

The impression was no less vivid in the mind of Harry (Bud) Grant, never renowned as a romanticist. They asked Grant about Jim Marshall a couple of days before. Among guardians of the English language, Grant is revered for his thrift with superlatives. But he said:

"We won't see another like him in our lifetimes. To understand the kind of game he played last week against the Rams you would have to sit in our film room. You would see a thirty-eight-year-old man going full bore from start to finish against one of the best teams in football, and not only against the man assigned to block him. They had a rookie quarterback so they gave him maximum protection by doubling on our defensive ends. They had a 270-pound tackle and a 230-pound back blocking on Marshall. He came charging on every play. I don't know how many times he ran the width of the field chasing a play. We had to substitute for practically everybody on the defensive team at one time or other, but Marshall was still going wide open at the finish. Our new defensive line coach, Buddy Ryan, came up to me after the game. Buddy has seen and coached a lot of the great ones around the league. He said, 'I can't believe this guy. I never saw anybody like him.'"

I have always looked on Marshall's stewardship with the Vikings as being less a career than a geological age. It has moved with that kind of rhythm, exacted that kind of attrition on what lay before, responded to obstacles by trusting to simple inevitability. This special geological age was supposed to end a few months before. Its extinction was assigned by nature to young Mark Mullaney, a likeable fellow from the mountains who was hired to replace Jim Marshall.

Mullaney did not replace Marshall in Detroit. Mark was injured. It wouldn't have mattered if he were healthy. Mullaney was not going to replace Marshall in 1976 in Detroit, in Baghdad or on the moon—wherever they scheduled exhibitions or the playoffs.

The waivers lists, football's graveyard, are dappled with the names of people who were going to unhorse Marshall in the Viking lineup or on the line of scrimmage Sunday. Next year? Why sweat next year, as Marshall surely would ask. He is not easy to explain medically, so the medical people have given up. At this time of his career, it's much more rewarding simply to enjoy Jim Marshall than to try to explain him. You can sit in the mouldering seats above the Viking practice field in Midway early in the season, lightly hypnotized by the autumn sun and the sounds and movements of these expensive little-boys-turned-celebrity with their size and speed and virtuosity. The bulls are working near the sidelines. Defensive linemen. The first man through the drills is a thirty-eight-year-old man, soon to be thirty-nine. He does the up-and-downs, dropping to the turf, jumping up, dropping again, time after time. The exercises would tear the muscles and cave the lungs of the average man, and they sometimes exhaust a football player. Marshall does them precisely and with unguarded glee. Why shouldn't he? This is Wednesday afternoon on a football field, and it is the universe for Jim Marshall. It is his spiritual nourishment and his physical renewal. It is the source of his youth and the renunciation of time.

He is vaguely invincible out here. As long as he wears his pads and birdcage, and ducks the raucous harpoons in the locker room each afternoon, he has his security.

His shrewder friends in the game have been admonishing him for years: "Look beyond today. Get yourself ready for a life without football."

He nods. He looks at them with big, soft, hazel eyes of gratitude. It's unmistakable. He digs. And then he says, "Hey, man. That's right." But when they are gone he puts the birdcage back on, and if you have very clear eyes you might detect a wry bristle in his mustache—and a wink.

Did they tell Bojangles he might not be able to dance someday?

Yes, I acknowledged in the press box, he has matured. For interviewers he now launches himself into untrackable flights of philosophy. Replaying them on their recorders, the interviewers find themselves grappling with water. Marshall might understand it all—but possibly not. His creeds sound mysterious and grand and terribly profound, but the logic in them often seems to sweep the listener majestically into oblivion.

But let somebody else be befuddled by Jim Marshall's earnest voyages into metaphysics. Maybe Jim embarked on them because he didn't like his reputation as the oldest adolescent on the varsity. Maybe he thought there should be something more dignified. He was usually cast as a man with exotic and reckless appetites, in constant peril of being struck by the flying pies of fate. Feeling patriarchal as he neared forty, Marshall rejected this portrayal as dated and defamatory.

Some who remembered him best from the early years regard his latter-day serenity as a dodge and hoax, maintaining that the real Jim Marshall was still the dreaming daredevil and sandlot sprite.

Why quibble? He never said the stars and abandoned gold mines had lost their allure for him. He just said he was getting older. But there was still a kickoff every Sunday afternoon in fall, and therefore Jim Marshall was still Jim Marshall. The real one was the instinctive one, hilarious, mournful. He never aspired to lead. The game itself, the delights of colliding and pursuing, horsing around with buddies—these were aspiration enough. He never hungered hard for the medals and eulogies that came with the passage of time. And yet in 1976 nobody on the Minnesota Vikings had more respect—and few if any had more in the entire pro football lodge.

His name rarely appears on the rosters of the accepted greats among defensive linemen. On his own unit of four, he has stood third for years behind Carl Eller and Alan Page in the collection of professional honors and public recognition. Until five or six years ago he was notable chiefly as a popular flake with a tendency to commit magnificent pratfalls such as running the wrong way, incorrectly swallowing a grape and accidentally shooting himself in his car. These often deflated his achievements and wrongly put Jim Marshall the uncommonly good football player in competition with Jim Marshall the notorious oddball.

But you can mention his name now to a Viking rookie, white or black, and there is instant registration, the recording of a value. It is the young player's appreciation of what it must have taken for a man to play eighteen years in this glamorized but heartbreaking game and still play as he did in 1976, with a yelping vibrancy that overlay an impregnable will. It was a quality built on struggle, wounds, an extraordinary body and comradeship.

Grant always said there was no price you could place on what Marshall meant to the Vikings. "You don't want to think of him as an institution, though," he said. "That implies something gray and humorless. The greatest thing about Marshall is that he never let the game get away from the playground. He's not the shrewdest player, but he wasn't constructed that way. He learned the game believing there's no problem that can't be overcome if you run at it hard enough. Gung-ho, that's his football. And if anybody believes pro football players are a bunch of cool dudes, they ought to listen to our locker room on Friday after practice."

In Marshall's corner the scene has all the calm and dignity of an Italian fish market. Marshall is chief custodian of a creative bedlam. He screams insults at Eller, Tarkenton, Foreman, defenseless newspapermen and other targets of opportunity. He rails and laughs, squeals and bellows, a 230-pound elf. Next month he will be a 225-pound elf. His weight dwindles as the season ages. In December he will weigh less than 220 pounds, a thirty-eight-year-old man no heavier than a linebacker, facing 270-pounders on the line of scrimmage. At such times he lies about his weight with a superb theatrical presence, as a matter of right and privilege, much as a mature Hollywood sex symbol will lie about her age. It's nobody's business what he weighs in December. It is the kind of information that may be used against a man, and he therefore ought not to be required to testify against himself.

Friday afternoon in the locker room is his ignition for Sunday. He is also perhaps declaring something subconsciously: that nothing on earth is better for Jim Marshall than the life of a football player with a big ball game coming. It helps to be healthy, but if his knees are aching or he's got a temperature, what the hell. Nobody said comfort was a requirement of the job.

His uproarious fantasy lives have waned, it's true. As a rising young ball player he decided what life needed most from Jim Marshall—what it virtually demanded—was a succession of dazzling deeds. He would be a skier, fortune hunter, wig salesman, mobile telephone salesman and film documentarian. With luck he could handle most of these in the same week. He plotted and dreamed, then leaped into action. He imagined these things as a boy in the ghettos, and most of them he achieved with zeal if not overwhelming skill. And they were not scatterbrained visions. He was honestly excited, and still is, by the next horizon, by tomorrow. One such horizon nearly killed him when it spawned a blizzard in the Beartooth Mountains. Its impact on his life seems to enlarge in retrospect. Its discoveries deepened his understanding of self and his humility in the face of forces that cannot be controlled, among them death.

It was intended as a motorized picnic in the high country, a passage by snowmobile over the two-mile-high Beartooth Pass between Red Lodge, Montana, and Yellowstone Park. I invited Jim on an impulse. For years we had hazed each other about a mountain climb together in the west. One of Marshall's phantom lives was that of a mountaineer. I told him to arrange a sabbatical in August some year. He said he knew of only one man who would object to such a worthy project—Bud Grant, who scheduled football practices in August. So we were never able to coordinate our time. But in the locker room depression after the Vikings lost a playoff game to Dallas in 1970, I thought I might relieve Marshall's distress by asking him to join our party. And because one of his locker partners had similar hungers for the high country, and similar despairs at the moment, I invited Paul Dickson, too.

There were sixteen riders and machines, a number well beyond my first intentions. It was a concession to appeals from friends of friends, including Marshall himself. There were too many, but the years of hindsight have now mercifully ended. The frolic turned into a horror. A ground blizzard struck the party near the summit, tearing it apart and leaving the machineless riders to grope down the mountain in the impenetrable night or to seek whatever shelter the screaming wind allowed. For three it was a shallow trench. Five others found sanctuary in each others' arms on the naked summit. One dug a snow cave.

Marshall and Dickson slogged for hours with three others, a fifteen-year-old boy, a professional snowmobile mechanic and a brave little woman, Marilyn Waples, the wife of a Red Lodge game warden and guide. In another era Jim Marshall and Paul Dickson could not possibly have known each other, let alone traveled together. Nor could they, in the transitory but authentic way of athletic teammates, have loved each other. One was black, a light-footed spirit out of the sunbeams and beanstalks of society. The other was a Texan driven by century-old concepts of the frontier, moody and independent. Yet they hit it off marvelously together. Because they were mavericks away from the regimentation of the playing field, they understood each other. They acquired the mutual respect that is the peculiar province of athletes who share pain and triumph along the line of scrimmage. The old notions of racism both knew in one form or another seemed, in the winter of 1971, a long way behind. They shared another thing: the liberation of roaming the hills.

38

When the crisis came in the Beartooth, neither affected any structured bravery as a professional athlete. When they had to, they stood up to the storm. But they didn't shrink from being led by a woman. This was Marilyn's country. She knew the way out of the hurricane-ravaged pass. And they were scared—which made the condition unanimous, because so were Marilyn and the others.

There were no secrets for them. As the ball players began to tire they did not try to hide from each other, or others in the party, their wonderment at the tough qualities of the pretty, 105-pound lady. They went on for hours, plunging to their chests in powdered snow at almost every stride. They were stronger, but it was more tiring for them because their weight worked against them; the others often were able to avoid breaking the crust. They gulped air and wheezed. Sometimes they prayed. When that wore off, they swore. Marilyn led for a while, but there were stresses on her the others did not have to cope with. Her husband was somewhere on the mountain, miles ahead, looking for shelter for the party or for help. Her children were back in the cabin in Red Lodge. As the storm, the miles of slogging and the anxieties drained her strength and attacked her will, she faced a truth she had been trying to suppress for hours: There was a strong chance she would die on the mountain on this night.

She was becoming queasy, and she didn't know whether the cause of it was her fatigue and hunger or her worry about her husband and children. Another candy bar might help. As she started to remove the wrapper, she fell and retched. She got up, but her teeth were clattering so violently it embarrassed her when the others came to help. She wanted to cry in her futility. But she started to walk some more, plunging to her knees in the snow despite her smallness.

Jim Marshall and Paul Dickson asked her to rest a few minutes. They were moved by the woman's struggle to keep herself under control and her unspoken refusal to do no less than the men. But she could not control her shivering or conceal her fears. There was no warmth they could give her but that of their bodies.

Together they wrapped Marilyn in their arms and held her. None of the three spoke; all had reason to be grateful to those they touched.

Then they turned back to the valley that lay somewhere in the night storm. It was mean and boisterous, a personal purgatory in the desolation and fatigue it inflicted on each. It was beyond midnight. They had been struggling for hours. Bobby Leiviska, the fifteen-year-old, was leading. Ironically, he was now stronger than the professional football players he idolized. Dickson was hallucinating. He saw sparks, he said. It must be from the chimney of Top of the World, a summertime souvenir shop that could give them refuge. But Top of the World was miles away, and there were no sparks. The glints of light Dickson saw were the stars flashing through the snags of wind-ripped cloud. What he thought were the eaves of buildings were mountain ridges.

Marshall thought he heard voices. But there were no voices. The sounds were the malevolent mockeries of the mountain gale.

There was no sound strong enough to ride four miles on the wind Jim Marshall believed was carrying his voice from the Top of the World to their stumbling little clan. Without knowing it, Marilyn and the others passed within twenty feet of where her husband lay recuperating in a snowcave beside frozen Long Lake.

They had to find a place. Another fifteen or twenty minutes of this and they would collapse. Bobby saw a grove of Douglas firs on a low ridge 400 feet off the route. He yelled to Marshall and Dickson that he was going into the trees to look for shelter. He discovered a glen, a small snow bowl surrounded by big evergreens whose snow-plastered branches reached a hundred feet into the air.

Within five minutes the five were gathered in this rough

40

sanctuary, wheezing but spirtually revived. The wind was spent. Overhead the cloud tatters had dissipated and the stars delivered a faint benediction.

They fell into each other in the snow and lay there for several minutes, too tired to talk but aware that if they could get a fire going, they would be safe for the night. Jim looked at the spunky fifteen-year-old sitting cross-legged a few feet away.

"Don't go to sleep, boy," he said. "See that fella on your shoulder? The Grim Reaper. Grim Reaper gonna get no one tonight. He ain't gonna get Jim Marshall. Only way he's gonna get Jim Marshall is across the cheeks of his hind end, because Jim Marshall's gonna be runnin'.

"May as well sit on my shoulder, Grim Reaper. No way you gonna get Jim Marshall or Bobby. Nobody. Ain't your night, Reaper."

It was a litany from the athlete's past, the folk superstition with which the old ones cowed the kids. There was something deliberately tribal in the way he said it. In his exhaustion and hunger the football player was in the ghetto again.

"Go away, Grim Reaper."

Dickson had his lighter out and was gathering sticks and wet pine needles. "How's that stuff gonna burn, man?" Marshall demanded.

Marilyn laughed weakly. The big fellows seemed restored. They were now amateur trailblazers haggling over how to build a fire. Marshall was right; the soaked green needles weren't going to burn. But they must have dry paper in their packs and clothes.

Marshall's hand emerged from his pocket. He tore open his checkbook and crumpled some blank checks onto the snow beneath one of the big Douglas firs.

Dickson couldn't avoid the temptation. "Is that paper, Marshall," he asked, "or rubber?"

"Man, you breakin' me up," Marshall said. "Light the goddamned fire."

Dickson flicked the little cogwheel against the flint. It flamed and the checks ignited. Marshall was ready with some candy bar wrappers. Dickson threw on some notepaper he carried with him. It burned too quickly; the tiny fire was dying. Jim Marshall fumbled in his billfold again. He came out with green in his hand: some twenty-dollar bills, some tens, some ones. The situation called for a nimble decision in high finance. Jim decided that a couple of one-dollar bills had the very same combustibility as a pair of twenties. He crumpled the ones into the little firebed, not without some fugitive remorse.

It was good currency of the realm. It burned.

They walked around looking for windfall they could rip into kindling. Bobby pulled down a branch from one of the firs, mumbling the boy ecologist's apology. Jim Marshall appointed himself fire tender. He cupped his hands over the timorous flames, protecting them from any antagonistic breeze that got between his bulk and Dickson's. He sculped the fire, nourished it and talked to it.

"You can't go out on us, baby," he counseled. "No way you gonna go out on us. We need you, baby. Melt those boughs, you hear? Way to go, fire."

The fire was going. They were going to live.

They hunkered around its deliverance. The fire succored their aching bodies and melted the ice goiters that had formed on the face masks beneath their chins. It sucked steam from their soggy mittens. They felt the flames burn away their anxieties. Mentally they applauded, declaring their thanksgiving and their juvenile delight at the fireworks of sparks flitting into the great wet branches overhead.

"Marshall," Paul Dickson's voice boomed into Jim Marshall's descending drowsiness, "I didn't actually believe those B. F. Goodrich checks would burn."

They all laughed. It was not a great gag line, but their mirth, and their relief, rang through the woods. The forest responded with its respectful silence, as though it understood.

It was the first time they had laughed, some of them realized, in more than twelve hours. The flames leaped above them, and the forest suddenly filled with goodness. They brought wood to feed the fire. They horseplayed and munched nuts from their pockets and Marshall's pack. Somebody dug deeper and produced a little chunk of cheese and a piece of salami. And then Jim Marshall went into his pack again. He came out with a revolver and a goatskin bag.

"They said we wouldn't need any firearms in this ·pristine wilderness," he said with his old mimicry. "I figured I might. Who knows what wild creatures might be at large." Dickson congratulated him on discovering a new self—Daniel Boone. The frontiersman in his billowing purple snowmobile suit now passed around the goatskin bag, containing what he described as "Jack Daniel's finest."

Nobody had to issue cautionary words. It was a freshener; it was also some kind of reward. But it shouldn't be anything more than that.

They could see the moon. And now, just before they began to yield to the sedation of fire and fatigue, anxiety returned. What about the others? Were all of them safe?

Two thousand feet above them, Bobby's father and Monte Later of St. Anthony, Idaho, struggled to save Hugh Galusha, a wise and gentle Minneapolis banker, a Montanan whose reverence for the mountain wilderness had brought him back one more time. Marshall and the others learned about his death when all were reunited hours later.

I remember Jim Marshall solemnly shaking my hand that evening, telling me about the others in his group. What were the snickers that trailed the Minnesota Vikings? They couldn't win the big ones, perhaps because of some disposition to clutch in the crisis, as though their veterans were afflicted with some character defect that made them cave in in the hour of deepest trial? Nobody would recognize the absurdity of this easy slander as quickly as Marshall's companions on the Beartooth.

Marshall played in his first National Football League game in 1960 after a year of Canadian football and three years for Woody Hayes at Ohio State. On the eve of his 225th, a newspaperman asked him what he remembered about the first game.

"I remember I was underweight, recovering from encephalitis and so nervous about it I didn't want my wife (then his fiance) to come watch," he said. "I didn't invite her to the game because I wasn't sure I'd play well, and I didn't want her to see me play bad."

And his extraordinary endurance? Did he have a body forged on Mars?

"People say I play injured more than some ball players, that I've got a higher pain threshold, all those things," he reflected. "I'm not a doctor. I know that playing football is a commitment with me. I love it and I crave it, and when I'm around it I'm content. If I'm sick, I play. If I get sicker, I still play. Got to. You don't want to get moved out of there. If it's your life, you play. I never broke down any doors of the gyms to stay in shape in summer. Some guys do. Everybody does what they have to. Me? I like music in summer. When I get to camp, I'm there to play. Everybody knows that. Nobody has to tell me football can't go on forever. But retiring never crosses my mind. I don't see why this has to be my last year. I always think that. I'll think that next year, too. There's all kinds of things you discover in this game. Carl Eller and me. We're into meditating now on road games. We just sort of bring it all together and get ourselves into a positive frame of mind, not only for football, but for life.

"People ask if I ever envied all the honors Carl and Alan have had, if there's any feeling of rivalry between us. There never has been. When you respect a man as a ball player and a human being, how are you going to envy what comes to him? I haven't been ignored, and even if I was, why cry? You get back just about what you invest in life, and I've tried to put as much as I can into it."

Approaching his 225th consecutive game as a starter in the world's most demanding football league, Jim Marshall still had not lost his appetite for the wind or for the line of scrimmage. He still relished his teammates' applause over some piece of burlesque on Friday afternoon.

And the answer for whether it was all worth it was in the eyes of his teammates, his opponents, his coaches and his friends.

From Jeff Siemon's journal

Wednesday, September 22   We know it's going to be a dogfight in Pontiac Stadium. The Lions will be screaming and hollering and doing everything they can to disorganize us. It's the Detroit style. Nobody exemplifies it like Charlie Sanders, their tight end, who is a great ball player but no angel on a football field. Most of the Viking defensive veterans have had confrontations at one time or another with Charlie Sanders. Not only in games with us but with most of the other teams, Sanders has been known as a blindside hitter. He has made some of the most vicious hits I've seen. I don't mean after-the-whistle hits or clipping. As a matter of fact, basically they're not illegal. But he's always catching the opponent unawares toward the end of a play, on a screen pass or a quarterback scramble. He delights in catching people off guard and coming up with a vicious forearm to the head or any place where he can do some damage.

Charlie caught my friend Mike McCoy of the Green Bay Packers in a situation like that. McCoy just turned to run after a screen pass when Sanders came out of nowhere and blasted him, cracking several of his teeth in the process. I watched films of the Lions-Bears games of last year. Sanders got the same kind of hit on Wally Chambers of Chicago and knocked him out of the game.

For years the classic battle has been between Charlie Sanders and Hilgenberg. Two years ago Wally caught Charlie coming over the middle, not looking. He threw a forearm and knocked Sanders dizzy. Wally was fined by the league and earned us a 15-yard penalty for that. I don't think the officials saw the play, but circumstantial evidence alone might have been enough to convict Wally. They have hammered at each other time and again, and I've seen Wally with a bloody nose and Sanders with cuts and bruises, and it's always a pretty grisly meeting when the two of them face off. Marshall always complains that Wally provokes Sanders just about the time Sanders is lining up to block the defensive end. Charlie is a tight end on offense for Detroit, of course, and the defensive end Jim Marshall is talking about is Jim Marshall. Marshall likes Sanders much better when Sanders is a calm dude on the football field. When he gets mad, he goes after people who happen to be in the way, and often Marshall is the guy.

We were watching films today and one of the coaches commented that Sanders didn't appear to be as belligerent as in previous years. Wally said, in the half-clowning, half-serious way in which he often looks at his football life in the middle of the week, "Don't worry, I'll stir him up and get him active again."

Marshall just hung his head and shook it slowly.

The Hilgenberg-Sanders carnage was not renewed at Pontiac on September 26; both players behaved with relative civility and only occasionally tried to gouge or dismember the other. Sanders, in fact, enjoyed one of his more exemplary afternoons against the Vikings: He caught four passes and scored a touchdown. But the shock of playing well against the Vikings suddenly impacted on him in the final minute, and he pulled a rookie blunder that he later claimed cost his team the game, 10–9.

Charlie failed to step out of bounds on a pass play during a last-breath drive that might have produced a winning field goal. But his misplay was smothered by earlier events, chiefly the Vikings' tardy processional from their hotel to the stadium.

They were quartered in the Northfield Inn, which according to Bud Grant's surveyors was not much more than fifteen minutes from the stadium under average before-game driving conditions. Travel time is a critical piece of mathematics for anybody on the Viking staff remotely connected with getting the ball club to the ball field. Grant determined years ago that the optimum time of arrival for his football team is one hour before the game. Let the other teams lounge in the dressing room for an hour; let the other guys yawn or grouse, read programs half-dressed, watch television or admire fan mail. Grant's warriors would stride into the room, dress crisply, run out for warmups, return for any terse wisdom required from the head coach, run back onto the field and stand impeccably for the national anthem. These controlled exertions developed a pace that Grant judged to be ideal for a football team readying itself for war. All its movements were conducted with a practiced, and therefore comfortable, briskness. The resulting mood was becoming to the pro athlete, Grant maintained. It was, in other words, the essence of professionalism.

There are many in the National Football League who twitter over these devotions of Bud Grant and the Minnesota Vikings. Most of them finish far behind Bud Grant and the Minnesota Vikings. Being out of the playoffs, they have time to twitter.

The catchspring for the whole process is the team's arrival time at the ball park. Grant allocates one hour (actually one hour and six minutes, allowing for the television pre-game and commercials) for all the team's chores before kickoff. The arrival of the bus an hour before game time eventually acquired the force of a prescription for the players and a mandate for the navigators.

A year ago the Vikings' bus had negotiated the almost identical ten miles in just under fifteen minutes, arriving at the Pontiac dome at 12:59 for the scheduled 2 P.M. kickoff. It was a logistics performance Grant considered good under the conditions.

The departure time for Pontiac was thus programmed into the Vikings blueprint for the weekend. Barring an act of God, no deviation would be seriously considered. Grant was never stern or authoritarian about it; he believed in having subordinates who made an intelligent assessment of the situation, used some of their own judgment, and then acted in about the way Grant would act. Rain fell in Detroit on September 26, but it did not fall heavily enough to earn the rank of a providential act. So the two Vikings buses left at 11:45 A.M.

Available statistics from the Michigan Highway Department indicate that approximately 80,000 people had the same idea at about the same time.

At the appointed arrival time the Vikings buses were still five miles from the Silverdome. In all the monumental history of traffic jams before gametime, this one might have retired the trophy. At 12:15 P.M., forty-five minutes before game time, the buses crept around two stalled cars believed to be the villains in this mass automotive malaise.

Safely past the stalled cars, the Vikings buses moved even more slowly. At 12:25 P.M., general manager Mike Lynn, riding shotgun in the second bus, disembarked and ordered the first driver to run on the grassy median. Sherm Pinkham, the Vikings administrator in charge of arriving at noon, also left the bus and, ankle-deep in mud, began directing traffic so as to give the two buses a little better angle of attack on the open slits of highway.

Nothing worked. Returned to the bus, Lynn began taking a fearsome roasting from the football players—some of the world's most merciless baiters.

Francis Tarkenton was generalissimo and all-around instigator. "Hey Lynn," Tarkenton yelled. "How about another pre-game meal? Your men are on the verge of starvation. You want this group to go into the Lions' den famished and suffering from rickets? Their blood will be on your hands, Lynn. How about stopping at the Dairy Queen?"

Tingelhoff, sitting in front of Tarkenton, pointed out that the bus was already stopped and couldn't stop any faster.

"How about sending out a runner, Lynn? Maybe we could launch a flare?"

Lynn raised his coat collar a little higher to conceal a temptation to shrivel.

Tarkenton renewed the bombardment. A wrenching chorus of "The Prisoner's Song" began to well from the back of the bus.

"Mike," he shouted. "We're not gonna have enough time to warm up and it will permanently wreck my arm."

"Your arm was permanently wrecked the first time you tried to throw 40 yards," Lynn mumbled, temporarily slowing his retreat.

48

"Listen to Milton Berle, gentlemen," Tarkenton howled. "Some of the highest paid talent in the world is on the verge of malnutrition, right here in this bus, and we're now going to get a fifteen-minute monologue from Milton Berle Lynn."

Aboard a car in an adjacent lane, large-eyed football fans peered into the bus. Hilgenberg opened a window. Not recognizing the occupants of the bus, one of the fans yelled to Hilgenberg: "I'll take the Lions and three points."

"So will I," Hilgenberg replied. "I don't think the Vikings are going to show."

"Lynn," screamed Tarkenton. "I'm going to sue. You're going to make me throw without a warmup, and it will wreck my arm and take ten years out of my career. I'll sue for millions."

Lynn pondered the prospect. "It can't be much more," he said, "than you're making right now."

Shortly after the appointed kickoff time, the Vikings buses arrived at the stadium. Freddie Cox, always the first assigned to the field, was removing his clothes before he hit the door. Seven minutes after he opened the dressing room door he was jogging onto the field with his holder, Paul Krause, to practice kicks.

The Lions' coach, Rick Forzano, struck a grandly humanitarian tone with 15 yards already in his treasury. "Make sure you're ready," he advised the Vikings. "Warm up all you need." Forzano delayed some of his own squad's warmups, which permitted the young Lions cornerback, Levi Johnson, to hear television's Jimmy (the Greek) Snyder announce that Tarkenton was going to pick on Levi Johnson this afternoon. "I intercepted the man last year," Johnson said gleefully, "and I'll intercept him again."

They finally kicked off at 1:30 P.M., some twenty-five minutes late, after the Vikings had warmed up for twelve minutes. Johnson got only meager chances to fulfill his vow. Early in the game Tarkenton was crunched by Lions linebacker Paul Naumoff, suffered torn rib cartilage and played the rest of the half in pain and under great duress. Dr. Donald Lannin and Zamberletti taped his ribs, and Tarkenton jogged back with the team for the

49

second half of a 3–3 game. He threw briefly on the sideline but was unable to deliver the ball more than 15 yards. Glumly he informed Grant, "I want to play, but I may get you beat the shape I'm in."

Grant ordered reserve Bobby Lee into the game and announced to the press box that there was nothing physically wrong with Tarkenton. There are many generous interpretations you can place on the coach's announcement, but when you finish with those you have to say it was just a plain and simple lie. Grant's rationale at the moment was perfectly forgivable; nobody had to know whether Tarkenton was hurt badly enough to affect the Vikings' personnel plans in the second half. In Grant's reading of the situation Tarkenton could have played (which was true). Therefore it could be said there was nothing physically wrong with him. It not only could be said, it was said. Television's Sonny Jurgensen put the only construction possible on it: Francis was being benched for ineffective play. Camera closeups seemed to support that thesis as they revealed the quarterback in an attitude of somber reflection, as though offended by somebody or something.

"I sure was," he said later. "I was offended by my bad ribs. They hurt like hell. What was I supposed to do, run around doing somersaults and giggling up a storm?"

With Tarkenton immobilized for one of the few times in his sixteen-year career, Bobby Lee quarterbacked the Vikings to a second half touchdown. Lee thus achieved his own kind of vindication out of the webwork of ironies strung by his presence as a replacement for Tarkenton. Five years before Grant had traded him to Atlanta, partly because of Lee's erratic performance in a playoff game against Dallas. His departure was dictated by Grant's preference for a quarterback then employed by the New York Giants, Francis Tarkenton.

Lee and Tarkenton faced each other in Atlanta in 1973, at a time when Bobby and Norm Van Brocklin were the delight of the new confederacy. Lee outperformed Tarkenton, Atlanta won, Van Brocklin triumphed over Tarkenton, and it was widely believed both Lee and Van Brocklin would be enshrined eventually with Stonewall Jackson and Jefferson Davis. The ceremonies were indefinitely postponed when the Falcons were upset twice in the final three weeks and blew a playoff berth. Van Brocklin was fired a year later, and in 1975 Bobby Lee was waived out of the league, too expensive at $90,000 to be wearing headphones on somebody's bench.

In September of that year the Vikings' Bob Berry, himself a former Viking who had to be liberated from Atlanta, maimed his foot. With a void behind Tarkenton, Grant reconstituted Bobby Lee. And he regretted it for most of the 1975 season because Lee did not adapt well to his old environment. Tarkenton rarely concealed his lack of esteem for Lee's quarterbacking. Grant nearly traded him in the off-season. But he would have regretted that, too, because in 1976 Bobby Lee vaulted past Berry and became once more an excellent NFL quarterback.

He may not have been excellent against the Lions, but he was good enough. Chuck Foreman scored the touchdown on an unorthodox draw play called in a burst of clairvoyance by Jerry Burns, the wise and noisy gnome who runs the Viking offense. The Lions got the touchdown back. But with a chance to tie, they disintegrated on the extra point. By the third game of the season the Vikings had already acquired a terrorist reputation for blocking kicks—inspired largely by Nate Allen, the emigre from the San Francisco 49ers, a reckless charger and a fellow filled with uncomplicated joys. Joe Reed, holding the ball for Errol Mann on the extra point, was worried about Nate Allen blocking the kick. That made it a threesome; Mann was worried, and so was Rick Forzano, the Lion coach who had been threatened with expulsion the previous week by Lions owner William Clay Ford.

The three of them might have been able to handle all that anxiety, but they didn't allow for a fourth, Lions center Jon Morris, who was worried by Alan Page, rooting and menacing in front of him.

51

So Morris centered the ball just a little high.

And Reed never got it down right.

And Mann never kicked it right.

And Nate Allen blocked it with a splat.

And the Vikings won, 10–9.

It surprised nobody that Jim Marshall should be awarded the game ball for starting his 225th consecutive game. It was the kind of day that might have encapsulated Jim Marshall's career. It had suspense, length, irony, a little bloodshed, a little misdirection, a victory for the just and two big tackles in crisis situations by the defensive captain of the Minnesota Vikings, Jim Marshall.

"I don't want to play forever," he said afterward, "I just want to play on Sunday."

Which may be the same thing.

4

A harmless part of the Super Bowl mystique is the way the games are numbered. The Vikings, for example, have played in Super Bowls IV, VIII, IX and XI. The use of the Roman numerals is intended to convey an epochal quality to the Super Bowl, a chiseled-in-stone character that permits each Super Bowl game to take on immediate historicity. You have to consider that a kind of miracle. It took other historic phenomena such as the Pyramids and the Great Wall of China centuries to achieve the same effect.

The Vikings have no such pretensions about their involvement in the Super Bowl. Since they have lost every one they played, they identify each by the team that won. The 1970 Super Bowl game, for example, they call simply "the Chiefs."

The 1975 Super Bowl game, then, was "the Steelers." Yet it was something more. In all their years of winning division and conference titles and losing the Super Bowl, the Vikings had never been as awed professionally as they were in New Orleans by the Pittsburgh Steelers. The score, 16–6, was presentable; so was the flow chart. The Vikings could easily have led at halftime and, from start to finish, their defense played responsibly, although it never found a solution for Franco Harris.

And yet, in their private evaluations of the NFL, the Vikings unanimously accorded the Pittsburgh Steelers a special rank, as though the Steelers should be playing in a higher league. Mostly this reflected their judgment of the Steeler defense—particularly the Steeler front four of Joe Greene, L. C. Greenwood, Ernie Holmes and Dwight White.

Tarkenton spoke of the Pittsburgh front four in terms previously applied to the Invasion of the Body Snatchers. "They engulf you," he said after the 1975 Super Bowl. "They are the best I have ever played against." He theorized later that if the Pittsburgh Steeler front four was transplanted to any mediocre football team in the NFL it could convert said mediocrity into a Super Bowl contender.

The Pittsburgh front four, supported by such non-mediocrities as Franco Harris, Terry Bradshaw, Lynn Swann, Jack Ham, Jack Lambert, Mel Blount and Rocky Bleier, accosted the Vikings in the first week of October 1976. It was a game the Vikings welcomed with minimal enthusiasm. They flatly believed Pittsburgh had the best team in football, and football included the Minnesota Vikings.

Yet the Minnesota Vikings won the Central Division championship, for all practical purposes, and steered themselves irrevocably toward another Super Bowl by flattening what was presumed to be the best team in football, 17–6. Allowing for the Steelers' mentality at the time—they were groping and thrashing with a 1–2 record going into the game, searching for a lost invincibility—the Vikings' Monday night performance will still stand among the five or six finest in the organization's history.

There is nothing in the standard player contract, however, that forces Monday night heroes to act heroically four days before the game.

From Jeff Siemon's journal

Thursday, September 30   Nobody's reputation is hallowed on the practice field. The offense has had trouble moving on the ground this year despite our 2-0-1 record. The defense was jabbing them sarcastically today. Page, Eller and Marshall were the chief prosecutors. Yary was in the dock most of the time for a newspaper story quoting him as saying the running game wasn't going very good now but would get rolling before long, if not this very next game against the Steelers. A couple of times the offense jumped offside. And Alan Page would say in an aside to Marshall, "Well, Jim, there's another five yards they got. They're really working at moving the ball on the ground." Somebody rolled the ball and said that was the offense's idea of rolling on the ground. It was really a piece of needlework, and you could see Yary's temperature rise about ten degrees between plays.

Yary wasn't the only guy to get hot on the practice field, as it turned out. It happened right near the end, when we were working on our field goal game for Pittsburgh. Fred Cox kicked a few and then Bud Grant came into the huddle and whispered that he wanted the kicking team to work a fake on the next play. I don't think we've run a fake field goal all year. And I don't remember ever running one in a game. Once in a great while we'll run one in practice to keep the defense alert.

Anyhow, Roy Winston was standing behind the huddle and evidently heard what Grant said or figured it out because just before the play was run Roy signaled Hilgenberg by giving him a look as though he was saying "watch a pass." He did a little more than that—he pretended he was throwing the ball. It was not a bad piece of espionage. About that time the ball was snapped, and Bud happened to catch Winston's act. Without looking, Grant flung the ball at Winston. Possibly joking. Possibly not. As fate would have it, the ball smacked Roy right in the face from a distance of 10 feet. Coach or no coach, accident or not, Winston was seething. So he let Bud know, in the way a ballplayer will. "If you didn't turn your head,"

Bud responded lightly, "the ball would have hit you in the face." To which Winston replied, this fellow who is actually a good friend of Bud's and an admirer and hunting companion: "It did hit me in the face, you asshole." Whereupon Roy threw the ball back at Bud.

It wasn't the kind of thing to break up a lasting friendship, though. Both of them recognized later it was just a practice field incident, although it did take Moony a while to get Bud back in perspective.

Saturday, October 2 It was a night of no sleep. I didn't spend it worrying about Pittsburgh. I spent it with an icepack on my thigh, and I was just miserable. Sometimes you can handle the enemy but can't do much about your friends. I was chasing after Robert Miller on a pass play today and all of a sudden I felt this fantastic pain. The tight end had run a similar pattern and at one point our paths crossed. Hilgenberg was chasing the tight end. I didn't see him and slammed into him. My left thigh just above the knee took the impact of Wally's knee. The pain was so bad I couldn't get off the ground for two or three minutes. So, two days before the Steeler game, I was up all night trying to hold the swelling down.

Sunday, October 3 I heard today that Bud said that my injury was just an old basketball injury, a thigh bruise, and I would definitely play against Pittsburgh. I know Bud has had a wealth of athletic experience, but it's hard to diagnose the severity of some injuries. Because there are people like Marshall, Winston and Eller who have played week in and week out with injuries, and played well with them, coaches and trainers—and even players—get into a dangerous habit of expecting every injury to be the same no matter how severe or how much time the players have had to treat it. This can be damaging because it puts a lot of pressure on the player to play, even if he will not be effective. That's really the key. It's fine to play with an injury as long as the injury doesn't expose the player to something worse, and as long as it doesn't hurt his team. In most cases the healthy guy you have on the bench is worth more to the team than a regular who is handicapped. I hope Bud is right, but I probably won't know anything for sure until a couple of hours before game time.

The little vanities of the big-time professional football player always amuse me, and I can laugh because I have some of them myself. It almost broke me up watching the players get ready for those pre-game closeups on television, where you give your name, position and home town. Bud has always taken a pretty hard line with the ABC Monday night show biz operation. He has no time for Howard Cosell, of course, and I understand he once threw Don Meredith out of the dressing room—which prompted Meredith's crack that if Grant and Tom Landry ran in a popularity contest, they'd finish in a tie for second. This time Bud said it was all right for our players to appear on the pre-game closeups, but they had to be shot the day before, when we were in street clothes—in other words, when we looked like normal people. He said shooting us right after the pre-game workout, when we were sweaty and unshaven, made us look like thugs. He said we ought to have a team decision on that, and of course the team thought Grant's idea was great and reasonable. Which is the way Grant works his peculiar democracy. But everybody broke out combs, hairdriers and hairspray, a whole cosmetic arsenal. Feminists who talk about macho attitudes among athletes should have seen that production. If anything, we were worse than women.

So far as I could see, nobody used makeup.

Monday, October 4 (before kickoff)   They have built a fiberglass device that will give my thigh some protection. I think I can play on it. I put some heat on it and did some stretching a few hours before the game.

The Monday countdown is interminable. Laying around. Talking. With me there's something extra this time, worrying about the leg. Two hours before kickoff I went to the stadium from our nearby motel and jogged a little. The ABC crew was already there, Frank Gifford and Alex Karras decked out in their brightly colored network jackets, going over some pre-game patter. A little after I started jogging I was aware of a familiar voice, sort of filling up the empty stadium with its booming quality and its demand for attention. It would be pretty hard to mistake Howard Cosell's voice in an artillery barrage. I'll say this: Howard didn't present any credibility problems. This was the same fellow and the same style from all the games I had watched on Monday night. The same self-assurance, sarcastic jokes, and arrogance, I suppose. A person doesn't want to judge too hard. People who know him tell me a lot of that is stage personality, the professional Howard. But others tell me the real Howard and the professional Howard are interchangeable. It's amazing, I'll say that, how he has managed to stir up so many people.

The thigh is okay, the weather is good. The feeling of tension, good, productive tension, is building. Sometimes you have doubts even when you feel good. Although Bob Lee is very capable, I don't know if we can beat this outfit with Tarkenton out of the lineup, but I do know we're going to come at them hard because they'll just wipe us out if we don't.

With 13 minutes of the game remaining and the Vikings leading, 7–6, Pittsburgh stood fourth and one on their 27-yard line. It had been an exasperating, physically jarring night for Terry Bradshaw, the Steeler quarterback. Somewhere here, late in the game, the Steelers would have to make a declaration. They would have to say they were the Super Bowl champions, that this was only the fourth game of the season and the molten steel pots in Pittsburgh weren't going to run dry if they gambled and missed trying to get over the hump. Fourth and one at the Steeler 27 struck Terry Bradshaw as an excellent time to make such a declaration. He called Franco Harris into the line, the best all-purpose running back in the world.

And then he looked across the line of scrimmage. Page, Sutherland, Eller, Siemon, Hilgenberg, Allen and the rest waited. They made no taunts, struck no melodramatic poses. They stood waiting for Franco Harris.

It was almost as though they were inviting him. If they had established anything in four weeks of the new season, it was a

58

tribal zeal in proving one of football's hoariest maxims: The last yard is the toughest. The Rams and Lions both had managed to end perfectly promising scoring drives by reaching the 1-yard line. There the Viking defense had suddenly altered character —both its own and that of the unsuspecting offense approaching the Minnesota goal line. The Vikings stopped the Rams there twice, and in Detroit they induced four straight downs of futility by the Lions less than two feet from the end zone. The memory of that, and the boomerangs the Minnesota short-yardage defense had inflicted on the Steelers earlier in the game, froze Bradshaw as he approached the line of scrimmage.

He is hardly a timid man. He had disclosed his texture as an athlete by absorbing pain and pressure in the Steelers' drive to the Super Bowl titles of the previous two years. But he now had no stomach for the Viking defense on fourth and one at his own 27. He called time and consulted with Coach Chuck Noll. They agreed it was not the ideal time for circus bravado. Thirteen minutes was an eon on the professional football clocks; there would be another time.

But there wasn't.

The Steelers decided to punt, intimidated not so much by muscle—they could certainly match that—as by the reality of the football game. They had been playing in disorder, snagged by penalties, blocked kicks, interceptions and the creative fervor of the Viking defense.

So they punted, and they lost the game. The center snap was high. Punter Bobby Walden was overrun by a purple ambush and dropped the ball. Nate Allen recovered at the Steeler 11, and two plays later Chuck Foreman's touchdown buried the Steelers.

It might have been stretching credulity to expect the horselaughing critics three months later, on January 9, to recall Terry Bradshaw's assessment of the Minnesota Vikings in 1976.

"I've seen a lot of great teams in short-yardage situations," he said. "I mean on the goal line and with less than a yard for a first down. But this was the greatest. They get so much penetration on you. They're tough and they're lean and they move. Against any other team on fourth and one we would have gone for it. What they were doing to us in that game, we couldn't go for it on our 27."

Nate Allen's playground impetuosity might have unleashed the juices for the Viking defense. Before it was over Nate had intercepted Bradshaw twice and recovered a fumble. Page blocked two placements and tormented Bradshaw without rest. The Vikings played defense with Nate's flamboyance, Page's instincts, Siemon's undemonstrative calm, Hilgenberg's recklessness and the timeless competence of Carl Eller and Jim Marshall.

The occasion ("the world was watching and it was time to assert ourselves," Eller said) gave them unity. They won by refusing the most minimal concessions to a football team that just a month before was compared with some of the mightiest in pro history. They would not allow the Steelers the simple courtesy of kicking the ball. Pittsburgh scored a touchdown, but Page stifled Roy Gerela's conversion. Gerela tried a field goal from the 22, and Eller blocked it. Gerela tried again from the 33, and Page blocked that one. With Page breathing hard in front of him, Mike Webster snapped one ball too high for Bobby Walden, and the Steelers blew the punt. To prove it could be done back-to-back, Webster snapped another high a little later under the same provocation. And Bobby, attempting to escape, fumbled the game away.

For Alan Page it was a tour de force on the part of one of the great football players of the time, one who claims in all seriousness that the exhilaration has gone out of football for him. He can't wait to escape his $100,000-a-year commitment to it so he can go into law. But his performance against the Steelers was a showpiece of his mechanical craft—and more. It was the essential Page, a two-and-a-half-hour statement that in a game of congestion, with twenty-two skilled and powerful people on the field, one man on the line of scrimmage can still control the game.

But don't the Vikings, according to the orthodox wisdom of the television screens, play all of their games with the emotions of satisfied barracudas?

"I played the game, and I guess I play every game, with a certain amount of fear," Page said later. "I'm not talking about fear of injury or fear of suffering pain or embarrassment, although sometimes that's present on the football field, and why should that be so surprising? The fear I feel, I guess, is the fear of failure. I know pretty much what my capabilities are, what I should be able to deliver, what's available to me and, if I don't deliver, what's the reason. Age? I'm thirty-one. I honestly don't think there's a thing I can't do today that I did when I was the most valuable player in 1971. The ego thing? It's there someplace for the pro football player. It has to be. It's the nature of the business. He's got to prove himself to himself over and over. So it's a trial. You get players who don't feel that way, or at least who say they don't. That's the guy who says, 'I've achieved. I don't have to prove that I belong in this position or that I deserve the recognition.' I think I have to prove it every Sunday. And maybe I worry about not proving it. Maybe that's what the coach means when he talks about intensity."

From Jeff Siemon's journal

Tuesday, October 5   Beating the Steelers, the way it was accomplished, the exposure of the game, all that made the game one of the greatest football experiences I've ever had. There were so many spectacular plays, Page's, Nate Allen's, Chuck Foreman's getting 148 yards, Bobby Lee coming through under the stress of replacing Francis in a critical game against the Super Bowl champion. It was great to see my good friend Nate Wright intercept one again after going through the 1975 season without one—a year that was a psychological struggle for him. And I intercepted one myself. I guess I had some severe pain in my thigh, but you feel it less on a night like that.

I suppose the play in the game I'll never forget was one overlooked by most people there. Toward the end Doug Sutherland peeled back

61

and absolutely demolished Terry Bradshaw on Nate Allen's second interception. I don't really know how Bradshaw got up from that, although I've seen him shake off so many shots and grope back dazed that I've got a picture in my mind of Terry limping and rolling his head and looking just devastated on his way to the bench. And then coming back the next series to throw the ball 60 yards. This shot was something else. It had to go down as one of the four or five most savage hits I've ever seen. Doug hit him with everything he had. Bradshaw's head snapped back and his whole body lurched and flew back a good five yards.

And then of course there was Nate Allen. I told Roy Winston when we traded for him that we finally had some depth in the secondary with Nate and Windlan Hall, who came over from the 49ers with Nate in the trade for Steve Lawson. You could see the first day that both of them were athletes, whether they played much for us or not. And they were going to give us different benefits, Nate with his eagerness and wide-open style, Windlan with his mental sharpness and versatility. What Nate has done so far is incredible. He gave us a win in Detroit by blocking a tying extra point. He saved us from a loss against Los Angeles by blocking Tom Dempsey's field goal. And now two interceptions and the big fumble recovery on Bobby Walden against Pittsburgh. How could a guy do more on the special teams? And Hall is the perfect special teams guy. He's willing to exert himself even though there may not be much glory in it—always thinking, always in the right place.

Tonight I started to think about the next Super Bowl for the first time.

For Nate Allen the game was the climactic hour of a month's voyage through the football cosmos, an Arabian Nights' fantasy fulfilled for the son of a South Carolina fisherman. Nate was a football vagabond whose new environment seemed now to clothe him in the cape of some rollicking supercreature. He blocked kicks, intercepted passes, knocked down 60-yard bombs, made open-field tackles, recovered fumbles. Each night he congratulated himself for the bounty of playing football with

Jim Marshall, Alan Page, Carl Eller and Fran Tarkenton. There is no way Walden or the Steelers could have escaped him. They could have refused to report for the second half kickoff, and Allen would have jimmied the dressing room door. They could have thrown the ball into the stands, and Allen would have been there in the second deck, carrying a butterfly net.

The day before he left the 49ers for Minnesota in the late summer of 1976, Nate Allen was subjected to the conventional nightmare stories about Minnesota winters. The prophet this time was Cedric Hardman of the 49er defense. "You're gonna freeze, Nate," he said. "Up there they wear earlaps on the Fourth of July. December, you're gonna look at the other teams and everybody is standing around the hot air blowers like they're pumping lifeblood. No hot air blowers for you, Nate. Oh, you're gonna like Minnesota."

Nate winked gallantly at Hardman. At the age of twenty-eight, with six years of good but largely faceless football behind him in the NFL, Nate could honestly admit only three things depressed him—cold weather, sitting on the bench and a day without laughs. If the Vikings wanted him, it meant they might have important plans for him. Nobody had to haul him screaming to a championship team. So it was cold in Minnesota in December? He had 11 months thereafter to thaw.

For his unforgettable one month, and several weeks thereafter, until he was injured and eventually unseated by Bobby Bryant, Allen played the Viking right corner full time. He played with gratitude and effervescence. He brought with him a quality Bud Grant called "aliveness" and which might also pass as rootin' tootin' gusto. He was full of bounce and repartee in the locker room, and on the corner he hit like a horse. Offenses might eventually uncover his lurking vulnerability to the deep pass—which they did in November—but he remained from start to finish in 1976 the core of a new ebullience that spread over these stylized men so renowned for their metallic discipline.

The old label was never a truly accurate fit; it couldn't be with a Marshall and a Hilgenberg in the ensemble. As a matter of fact, it was a bad rap. The Vikings were as capable of harboring squirrely characters and free spirits as some of the others. When they played for Grant, however, they suppressed some of these impulses in the interests of Grant's by-the-numbers professionalism and in the larger interests of staying on the payroll.

Nate Allen, with five years' exposure to the breezy atmospheres of the Kansas City Chiefs and the San Francisco 49ers, did not memorize all of the blue laws at once when he joined the Vikings in mid-October. Somebody blocked a New York Giant punt and Nate Allen picked it up. Dashing 28 yards into the end zone, Allen lifted the football and, in the pure ecstasy that seems a special endowment of great artists, children and black athletes, flung the ball into the end zone turf.

In any other stadium it was an act that would have merited scant recognition; triumphant athletes have been doing it for years. But not at Metropolitan Stadium.

Bud Grant views spiking the football as rank grandstanding and a potential hazard to the ballclub's competitive health. Some guy might make a mistake and spike the ball on the 3-yard line. Even more heinous, it was unprofessional.

And there was Nate Allen of the Minnesota Vikings, in God's natural sunlight, spiking the football.

Hundreds sat mutely horrified. A few of the more religious crossed themselves in dread. Some expected Nate Allen to turn into a snail. Magnetically, the eyes of the multitude turned to the Viking bench, where the man who holds the snail-converting franchise, Harry P. Grant, stood regarding the horizon. His view was obstructed by the scoreboard, which at the time read Vikings 10, Opponents 0. Under the conditions Grant decided against any rash act. Later he said he lost sight of Nate as he crossed the goal line. He saw, therefore, no evil. In the Viking system of crime and punishment, this meant there *was* no evil. There would be time later to lecture Nate Allen on the immorality of spiking the football. How was Bud Grant going to intrude his cool, gray logic on Nate's soaring heart after the ball game?

"Call me Nate the Trashman," he was chattering. "I pick up blocked punts, rolling footballs, hand-me-downs, anything they don't want to nail down or paint or kick in the end zone. I'm not particular. All I am is available."

From Jeff Siemon's journal

Thursday, October 7 I was so tired on the first day of practice for the Bears game that after eating dinner I went into the bedroom with the children and played on the bed for awhile. And when they went to bed around 7:30 I talked Dawn into lying down with me so I wouldn't feel guilty about dozing off at eight o'clock.

I've begun meeting with two high school boys, an idea and a hope I've had for a long time. I've wanted to get together with two fellows who had a genuine interest in studying the Bible and sharing with an older Christian. I conveyed this to Ron Davis, a fine young pastor in the Twin Cities area and one of my closest friends, who in turn directed me to the youth pastor who has been counseling the young men. They were unaware they were going to meet a professional football player. Craig Osborne, the youth pastor, never told them who was going to be discipling them, simply that he was a twenty-six-year-old man. It has begun as a strong and believable relationship, not dependent on my being a football player or somebody these fellows can look up to, but simply a relationship between a Christian man and two teen-agers who would like to pray with him and learn with him and perhaps draw from some of his experience in the world.

I had come to a point where giving my testimony to large audiences was less rewarding, and I wanted to spend more time with some of those faces I had seen in the audiences. I honestly don't believe they are aware of how much benefit it is to me. I just haven't had the personal contact with young Christians that gives larger significance to my needs to teach and to share. Christianity involves

65

commitment, and not only to Christ. As we are committed to Christ, the logical extension is a commitment to individuals. If we truly love people, we are willing to be committed to them. It's such a thrill for me to see tangible results. The time I've spent with these two high school people has given me exactly what I have prayed for and desired for years.

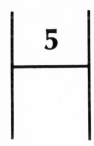

5

The spectacle of a man of Christ enmeshing himself in a world where people tear and bludgeon each other's bodies for money intrigues amateur sociologists and fans alike.

In other words, is there room for God on the 50-yard line?

At twenty-six, with five years of professional football behind him, Jeff Siemon has encountered variations of this question hundreds of times. At the very beginning his life as a professional athlete in a violent sport and his Christian belief never struck him as being contradictory. In time, however, he recognized that the question implied something beyond the simple peace vs. strife concept and perhaps something more sensational in the split-personality picture it seemed to conjure. It may have been tied to the position he plays. Didn't you have to be mean and ruthless to play middle linebacker, and what was a Christian doing in that kind of crowd?

At the time professional football was acquiring its popularity as both national escape and national fixation, the position of the middle linebacker was planted in the television watcher's mind as the place where carnivorous creatures dwelled.

It began with the portrayal of a New York Giant player

named Sam Huff as the personification of professional football's violent world. The country was ready for imagery like that; it was undergoing a mounting excitement and curiosity on Sunday afternoons. But the game was complicated, and the figures were none too recognizable. The picture of a Sam Huff both provoking and surviving a mayhem of swirling bodies simplified pro football as pure theater. Although he was good enough at his craft to win attention alone, Sam soon was accorded a status that took him into another dimension of public recognition. He became an archetype. Middle linebackers lived tough, dangerous and concussive lives. They were belligerent and shrewd. They were willing to walk into the jaws of an ambush and just as willing to create one. In time the psychological profile of the middle linebacker came to reflect in equal parts the spirits of Captain Kidd, Dracula and Heinrich Himmler.

The original model may have been Bill Pellington of the Baltimore Colts. Pellington considered it a day misspent when the rival center left the field with all of his natural teeth and his normal complement of blood. The role was lifted to its ultimate refinement of intimidation and show biz villainy by the Chicago Bears' Dick Butkus. Many NFL players insist that, in addition to being graced by these qualities, Butkus was the best middle linebacker ever. He was, in short, brutal, crafty, obnoxious, showy and great.

The advance of civilization in the last ten years and the toll of 15-yard penalties caused brutality to slip into disrepute. The best linebackers in recent years have been players who either by nature or the design of their team's defenses are wide-ranging yet disciplined players capable of meeting both pass and run with force and intelligence. Even more than some of their predecessors, they become the fulcrum of their defenses, assigned to seek out the point of attack. Among these were Nick Buoniconti of Miami, Lee Roy Jordan of Dallas and Willie Lanier of Kansas City. Bill Bergey of the Philadelphia Eagles and Jeff Siemon of the Minnesota Vikings entered the same general category in the middle 1970s. Jack Lambert of Pittsburgh, on the other hand, was a slimmed-down Butkus. Siemon played a much more structured game, except for his ability to drop deep in pass coverage. But his distinction as a linebacker lay not in his style or versatility but in the personality he brought to it.

Give me linebackers, coaches used to say (many still do), who are ornery and shovy and hostile. They ought to holler a lot and kick backsides—their own guys' backsides as well as the other guys'.

When Jeff Siemon joined the Vikings in 1972 the backsides in front of him belonged to Carl Eller, Alan Page and Jim Marshall, and the ones around him belonged to the likes of Wally Hilgenberg and Roy Winston. Discretion alone would discourage a Stanford rookie from molesting such venerable and sturdy backsides. But he has never been that kind of leader—if leadership can be defined that way—and never will be. It would be conduct alien to his character, to his perception of other people and to his witness as a Christian.

Is there such a thing as a Christian way to deliver a blindside tackle or a cut-block or to bury a quarterback in his own end zone?

To this Jeff Siemon will smile, a cautious though genuine smile. The question is a harmless rib. He acknowledges that.

"You can play the game hard and for keeps, and hit your opponents that way," he said, "and there's nothing un-Christian about that. I hate to see a player try to hurt, maim or humiliate an opponent. I'm convinced the Lord wants me to stay in the game of football as long as I can maintain a respect for my opponents and I am in control of my emotions. There are few saints in football, and I'm not one of them. But I don't play mean or malicious football. I really don't know many players who do.

"I do think there is a Christian way to approach the game and the people in it. There's one thing we all have in common, isn't there? It's called imperfection. I've never taken a lofty view of myself or felt a superior morality. That would be silly. But if in things I do and say, people around me gain a respect for a Christian faith, then I've succeeded in being the human being

I want to be. The greatest example I can give is to show respect for my teammates and to be genuinely interested in them, to be their friend. But a person can't do that alone. He's caught up in his own life and his own problems. For that he needs help, and he asks Christ to intervene on his behalf, to make his life an example.

"There are things I hear and see in a locker room that bother me because you would hope that as we find out more about ourselves we don't have to play those he-man games, to protect egos and to talk about sex exploits. But then you remember that the locker room really isn't a normal environment and that when you go one-to-one conversationally with a man who is boastful in a crowd, you often find that he is much more sensitive and respectful of others. In other words, he is a better person away from the demands of his ego."

Siemon is obviously a formidable young man, a football player of magnitude who commands important money and occupies a mounting visibility in his profession.

The chances that the profession offers for capitalization are huge. The pro football star today enjoys a name-and-face recognition once reserved only for movie idols and a handful of politicians. And yet Siemon behaves and talks—and observes his special ministry—essentially as he did when he arrived at the Viking training camp in Mankato. He was an All-American college football player who three years before underwent a conversion that has directed his life since his freshman year at Stanford.

Life had no mysteries for Jeff Siemon at his high school in Bakersfield. He was the son of a Bakersfield doctor, a popular and supersuccessful athlete, *the* cog on campus. It came easily, and as a teen-ager he discovered somewhere that the virtues of hard work were probably overrated. Not everybody knew him as a Stanford freshman, but there would be time for that. College was going to be Saturday afternoon in front of 90,000 people, the Big Game with California, the Rose Bowl. Weekend parties were not entirely to be shunned if you earned them with well-publicized heroics on Saturday afternoon.

But it didn't quite harmonize that way at first. Jeff Siemon was getting lost. He was badly outpointed in some of the classrooms and overlooked elsewhere. He searched around for some new entry into the life of a popular campus figure but found himself uneasy and adrift. He also found himself in the hospital, the victim of a serious football knee injury.

It was at that point in his life when he realized that his whole concept of worth and self-esteem was integrally tied to his success as a football player and student. He now came to see these values as shallow and temporal, ones that could be quickly and irrevocably snatched away. As a matter of fact, they had been. The life of achievement for the campus hero had skidded into frustration and melancholy.

He overheard a conversation one morning in his dormitory between his roommate and a young man from a campus Christian organization. He listened casually at first, then with mounting interest. Before the visitor left the room he confronted him with some questions.

"By the time the conversation ended," Siemon recalls, "I learned and understood for the first time that God loved me and accepted me as I am, a failing and inadequate Jeff Siemon. I understood that God could come into my life in the person of Jesus Christ, and to give it new purpose, direction and consistency. He could imbue me with a lifestyle that no longer had to be subject to the temporality of peer-approval but could now be based on the forgiveness and acceptance of a loving God.

"And that very morning I bowed my head and said, 'Jesus, I don't know what in the world you have planned for me, but I've run my own show for eighteen years and I've failed miserably. I ask you now to come into my life, to forgive me of my sin of indifference to you, and to make me the kind of man that you intended me to be."

The young man stabilized, became a student in fact as well as in name, a Christian activist, and an award-winning linebacker whose play climaxed in successive Stanford upset victories over Ohio State and Michigan in the Rose Bowl.

In Minneapolis, Bud Grant assembled his intelligence reports in preparation for the 1972 college draft and decided without reservation that Jeff Siemon would be his first draft choice. He was the kind of football player upon whom a coach, especially one with Grant's priorities, could build a team. At the critical defensive position of middle linebacker a coach wanted a man of strength and range. He should have intelligence, instinct and tackling aggressiveness. He should be able to perform deep drops on pass defense and be agile enough to move to the outside in lateral pursuit. He should have both the will and the ability to make the so-called big or game-turning plays that so much govern the results in any arena. (This is particularly true in pro leagues where so much pressure and prestige are involved and the competition is so tightly drawn.) He should be an organized man, one who wasn't dominated by demands for personal fame. And he should also be sound physically so that through an amalgam of all these properties Grant's middle linebacker could meet the twin requisites the coach considers the fountainhead of success in football: durability and consistency.

And it would not injure Grant's feelings if such a player could carry himself with dignity, valuing his own and respecting another man's. If he could find a middle linebacker with these qualities, let the inspired gorillas play for the other team.

Few (if any) players in Grant's recollection of twenty years of professional coaching have come as close as Siemon to achieving that composite. "It doesn't make Siemon the best player we have had," Grant will say. "But it does make him an exceptional one. He has a probing mind. He plays and lives with great awareness. In life and on the field he knows fully where he is going. He is very much his own person. He won't let himself be pressured into saying the easy thing or popular thing, or doing something because some code or team urgency seems to demand it. He may know that we'd like to see him try to overcome an injury and get back into action. Sometimes a ballplayer is subjected to great psychological pressures that way. Siemon is just not going to play until he thinks he's ready. There are a lot of players who wouldn't be so deliberate about it. But that's Jeff. He's got his own codes and convictions. No amount of peer pressure is going to hurry him."

He was going to feel such pressure acutely two months later, in a way that would arouse him to a rare outcry of anger. But however he got there, on his own volition or through the peculiar therapy that a big game exerts, he was on the field when his team needed him the most.

His mature carriage and obvious physical skills spared him any real awkwardness from the beginning, though he did feel some surface stickiness as a rookie middle linebacker breaking in on a team crowded with much-decorated football veterans— and headstrong veterans at that. He was not required to lead the team emotionally, and he would have been an imposter to try. He brought to the team a stability and bearing that attracted early respect quite apart from his ability. He was a big man, six-foot-two-and-a-half, 235 pounds, with a taut and powerful physique and a face that conveyed purpose and force. It was rugged, honest and firm from jaw to nose to forehead. When he spoke to his elders on the team, or to the coaches or to strangers, it was usually with a kind of civil solemnity. His eyes were settled and looked squarely into the other's, sometimes searchingly. In his first encounters with people he seemed austere. It wasn't Siemon's manner to be instantly chummy with anyone.

He has broadened since and acquired a warmth that was not evident then. He smiles sooner, and he is more deeply involved with the football team in a purely human way. His mind is constantly inquisitive. He will talk football, Christianity, the large and small phenomena of the world around him, team politics or the competing moralities of capitalism and socialism. In conversation on a team flight he is an incorrigible debater when he is not reading religious philosophy or playing cribbage with his roommate, Fred Cox. He once spent an hour in a hair-splitting semantic discussion with teammate Fred McNeill over the definition of time.

The coexistence of Siemon and McNeill as Viking linebackers is a study. Siemon is a declared Christian, although he's not overbearing about it. He is a family man and a human being rigidly under control who has few indulgences. McNeill, like Siemon, was a superb college player on the West Coast, having starred at UCLA. He is an engaging and intelligent fellow, black, totally fearless and aggressive on the football field. But his huge promise thus far is largely unfulfilled because of injury and an uneven graph of performance. Privately he is a popular bachelor with the conventional appetites, and yet he has an apparent yearning for a stronger, more comfortable identity. Several times in 1976 he seemed on the verge of asking Siemon's counsel. He seemed curious about Siemon's faith and that of those who formed the Viking prayer circle, Nate Wright, Amos Martin, Wes Hamilton, Robert Miller, Fred Cox, Ed White, Paul Krause, Matt Blair and others. Several more would drop in from time to time on Sunday mornings or Saturday evenings, Chuck Foreman and Carl Eller among them.

Siemon saw Fred McNeill's frustration over his progress as a football player. Sometimes he sensed personal ambiguities in Fred. He liked McNeill and he wanted to be a friend in a more personal way. Yet now and then there would be an incident.

From Jeff Siemon's journal

Friday, November 5   It was just a friendly $5 bet, but somehow it assumed an importance it shouldn't have. We were working today on some Detroit Lions blitzes, which we're expecting them to use 70 percent of the time on Sunday. Our defensive team was running the blitzes to familiarize the offense.

I checked the play sheet Neill Armstrong, our defensive coordinator, was holding. It appeared that Detroit's strong-side linebacker, played by McNeill, and the middle linebacker, played by me, were

74

supposed to loop. That meant we would work a synchronized pivot and shift the direction of our charge. Fred didn't loop, but I did, as I had seen the play drawn up. I got lost in the shuffle and ran into somebody, which gave my sprained thumb a really bad whack. I mentioned to Fred that he ran the blitz wrong. Fred said he ran it the way it was drawn, and I disagreed, saying I was pretty sure he was wrong. He asked me, courteously enough, whether I wanted to bet $5 on that. Off the cuff I said yes.

On the next down, after we had blitzed again, Fred asked me to show him the sheet containing the disputed play. Sure enough, the blitz had been drawn up two different ways. Fred had run it the way Armstrong wanted. But there was another way to run it on the diagram, and that was the way I had run it. So Fred said, "you owe me $5." I said no, it was drawn two different ways and we were both right. Fred said that that wasn't the bet, that I had bet that Fred was wrong. He started ribbing me a little about it and, as usually happens when I'm involved in one of these hassles, Fred jabbed me about my so-called high moral character. I could have predicted it. Whenever I get into something like that with a teammate the subject of my morality and Christianity inevitably comes up, mostly in a needling way. People like to probe that way, to remind you that all of us have thin skins and vulnerabilities, even those who claim to be living a Christian life.

While it is done in fun on the outside, I think underneath there is a kind of testing to see how I will respond. I look at my conduct in life this way: I am free from obligation and free from having to live a moral life for the salvation that God has given me. I know that he has forgiven me not on the basis of what I have done or not done but because of my faith in Jesus Christ and what he did. And if I understand this loving act of forgiveness, my response should be to live the best kind of life. In other words my acts, my lifestyle, should not be one of obedience to a chastizing, judging kind of God but one of obedience to a loving father we want to please.

I think God wants that kind of response. I say these things to explain how I react to the kind of testing a Christian must expect. This testing does not necessarily come from evil or malicious people.

Certainly it didn't in Fred's case. He was curious: How does this man of religion handle a $5 bet and explain himself when he gets pressured a little about it? And in reaction to this I try to do and say the things that in my mind uphold the teachings of Christ, in my own body and person. The next day I paid Fred the $5. No words were said. It wasn't easy to do, because I really believe it had become a no-bet situation. But I knew it was the best solution, and Fred accepted it. I didn't think I owed it to him, but the circumstances were such that it was worth $5 to restore an easy relationship between two players.

His teammates constantly appraise this unusual Christian jock who affirms a loving creed and moral ethic amid the locker room trappings of glamor, money and vulgarity. The appraisal is not always carried on openly. A few of Siemon's teammates, the older ones, respect his abilities and his beliefs but—perhaps because it is human to seek imperfection in others to make us more comfortable with our own—they see some hypocrisy in him. It is fine to live a life of fidelity and to worship God, they say, but why preach the Christian virtues and then take such a lively interest in the romantic habits of some of your teammates? One of them, now an accomplished wencher, privately accuses Jeff Siemon of being a gossip.

This induces a Siemon smile. "If you look at Christians and not the person of Christ," he said, "you will always see hypocrisy. I have forever believed that if I'm in fact free from immoralities in my own life, it is only because of the grace of God. I have never demanded that a teammate live up to God's standard of morality, because I myself can't. That's what forgiveness is all about. One of my weaknesses has always been an inquisitive mind, and it has gotten me into trouble more than once. We all have names for each other when something about the other guy bothers us. If I have been interested or talked with friends about a player's conduct, it's in the context of what the player seems to be doing to himself. The players on this team know I'm not a screaming evangelist. I don't go about claiming any kind of personal nobility. If a player shows a curiosity or an interest in what I profess, I try to respond.

"I don't know of any more rewarding thing on earth than Christian fellowship, both informally and through the Fellowship of Christian Athletes. We have a good deal of that on the Vikings, as most professional football teams do. It in no way has to mean any kind of clique or elitism. Just the opposite. It is an invitation. It is a way.

"I never look at a teammate on the basis of whether he is a Christian. To begin with, I think it is very difficult for a man to reach the NFL level of competition without having some special qualities of inner strength to go with his abilities. So I respect that. And you can't live for five or six months with people like Jim Marshall, Carl Eller, Jeff Wright, Nate Wright, Fran Tarkenton, Ed White, Alan Page and so many others without seeing so much there that is good in a human way, whether in a crisis on the football field or in the world outside the stadium. There is something about the bond of teammates that deters you from any rigid taking-of-inventory of all their qualities. It does become a kind of love, because their cause is yours. You don't have to hate the opponent to feel that. You understand your teammates' sacrifices, and you treasure the times they came up to you when you were doing badly or were hurt."

And so Jeff Siemon makes no attempt to proselytize in the locker room. He is an active worker in his faith without projecting piety. The pro football dressing room brings together personalities of a dozen social and spiritual urges. There are carousers and churchgoers, mixers and loners, extroverts, nervous Nellies, average neighborhood guys and prima donnas.

You cannot set out to impress such a variegated clan; the pose would be discovered and exposed almost instantly. "If you want to demonstrate a Christian attitude," Jeff Siemon said, "being honest about yourself and thoughtful of others are two ways to do it."

His unsentimental candor has become part of the club's lore. Four years ago Fred Cox, his roomate and a member of the

Fellowship of Christian Athletes, kicked an immensely high last-second field goal that beat Dallas. The Cowboys insisted the ball was outside the upright, an arguable point because the ball had sailed ten feet above the upright. "Ask Jeff," Paul Krause, the holder, told an inquiring reporter. "He'll give you a straight answer if he saw it."

Siemon's square, solemn face considered the question. "From where I was watching," he said, "the ball just missed. That doesn't mean it missed. It just means from where I stood it looked wide."

The National Football League, already familiar with Jeff Siemon's candor, needed to hear no more. The next year it added a fifteen-foot extension to the uprights.

"All it means," Cox said later, "is that Jeff won't have to agonize any more decisions on my field goals. There was nothing wrong with his honesty in Dallas. It was his eyesight. He was three inches off. Middle linebackers get that way after they take enough shots in the helmet."

Siemon handles this kind of razzing with ease and good temper. He welcomes it. Although he never felt he had to establish a breezy sociability to win acceptance in his earlier years, he realized that his sober exterior could be read as detachment or aloofness. He didn't feel that at all—and this, again, was part of his Christianity. He talked with ball players about God and faith and redemption whenever they showed a curiosity or wished to share a fellowship with him. But he also talked about blitzes, taxes, the death penalty and the price of coffee—or a baffling call by one of the coaches. With the rarest of exceptions he doesn't use four-letter words and he rarely raises his voice, but he is very much a citizen of the real world and a linebacker for a professional team in addition to his conducting a mission.

He did that from the start, and it has occupied him increasingly because a dynamic or so-called radical Christianity imposes that duty on him. He involved himself early in the Fellowship of Christian Athletes, an organization of high purpose and distinguished membership but suspect among some of the earthbound pros because a few of its members have gone to chapel Sunday morning after shacking up with a football groupie Saturday night.

This objection brings another wan smile from the middle linebacker.

"I would be dumbfounded to learn there isn't some sin in all of us," he said. "None of that discredits what the Fellowship of Christian Athletes intends to do and has done. It brings together athletes in a fraternal celebration of their faith, setting aside a time when they might share and question and declare their commitment to Christ. I have seen it give meaning to so many people and to comfort and enrich. If there are members in it who don't always live by its principles, what you are saying is that they are like all of us and are destined to fail."

From Jeff Siemon's journal

Friday, October 15   We had Bible Study last night. Ron Davis had a commitment and couldn't be there, so we had an unstructured group. We didn't try to recruit people who might have been lukewarm about coming because this was going to be a question and answer session and you had to want to participate. Wes Hamilton, Amos Martin, Robert Miller and Nate Wright and their wives were there, the regulars, along with Tom Reid of the Minnesota North Stars hockey team and his wife. The group was small, but sometimes this can give you a wonderful feeling of closeness, and we had that. Much of our talk had to do with the need for daily spiritual nourishment if we want the constant direction that God can provide for us. If we need food and water every day to maintain us physically, we need daily prayer and the word of God daily to sustain us spiritually. That shouldn't be idle rhetoric. We reminded ourselves how much deeper our lives were by putting that principle into practice. As we talked we all discovered that it's a common problem with all Christians, to put off and put off getting together in a quiet time with God each day. It's so easy to say "I'm busy today and I'll do it tomorrow." The meeting motivated all of us to be more firm about finding the time or making the time. We asked ourselves: What do you really do in the day that's more important?

His quests gradually moved Siemon into a whole congress of Christian organizations appealing to the activist. He gave his testimony both in public and privately one-to-one, which he preferred. He preached a Christianity of involvement. He shared both with wealthy Christians who had befriended him, such as Pennsylvania millionaire Art DeMoss, and with dying boys in hospitals who wanted to meet a real professional football player before they hurt too much to recognize him.

His idea of Christianity was to identify. The people he met and who sought his counsel saw him as an unusually self-sufficient man, seemingly without burden. He told them it wasn't that way at all, that he, too, had problems, fears, moments of meanness. And so they could talk together. He has tried to be a compassionate man, but one principle he pursues stubbornly is not to yield to humbug attitudes or phony shows of concern. A man whose writings have influenced Siemon is an Englishman named Os Guinness, whose statement of one side of the Christian attitude reflects Siemon's own behavior—one that is sometimes misunderstood because of the absence of runaway zealotry in everything he does.

"It is the very strength of Christianity," Guinness wrote, "that allows it to be gentle without being sentimental, tender without being trite, sacrificial without being melodramatic. Such compassion is not a front, nor a public relations exercise, but an expression of the heart of Christianity."

The passage might have defined Siemon's own focus as both man of his world and believer. He sees a responsibility to counsel and to be a friend, to be a member of a team and a part of the crowd, but he has never lost sight of his individuality or of the fact that there is a time to assert it.

If he believes a football coach is not a medical doctor and lacks clinical powers to diagnose an injury, he will listen to the coach but trust his own judgment on his readiness to help his team. Is this a form of self-importance? And is it a rationalization of a player's refusal to "suck it up and get out there," as the pros would say?

Not likely. It is simply Siemon. He challenges assumptions. He has to be satisfied. If he tries to be frank in his judgments of the small follies around him, he is just as frank in his judgment of himself.

From Jeff Siemon's journal

Sunday, October 10   We have beaten the Bears, 20–19, but we finished the game practically in disgrace. It's hard to believe we were tearing them up in the first half, 17–0. I remember telling myself on the sidelines that that should dispel any jittery feelings among our fans about the 1976 Vikings. And then everything flip-flopped in the second half, and before Walter Payton and the Bears' offense had finished we were right on the brink of panic. Nobody really knew how to stop them. I know I didn't have the faintest idea. I think it was the worst half of football I've played all year and one of the worst I've played in my life. The statistics credited me with a dozen tackles and some more assists. But when you look at the requirements of my job, the reading of keys, the making of open field tackles, filling holes, I don't think I could be much worse.

Payton had something to do with it. For a man who can run with power, I haven't seen a quicker back in my years in pro football. He's got tremendous strength, and a great toughness to make something happen every time he carries the ball. He bounces and hits, squirms, does anything he has to do. He gained 141 yards against us and he played so hard he just ran himself out—literally. They benched him the last five minutes or so, when they had a chance to win. I think if he had been on the field at the finish, they would have won. We were that disorganized.

The crises of pro football tend to recede quickly when there is a Monday morning of standard length and healing power. It is only after Super Bowl defeats that Monday mornings hold no therapeutic relief and sometimes last for weeks. Siemon's Monday mornings were usually free from grueling personal post-mortems. Whatever private searching he had to do fit conveniently into a quiet Sunday night, when Dawn helped.

They were married in Hawaii, the home of her parents. They return frequently, and they treasure it so much they named their second child, now three years old, Maile, which identifies a particular Hawaiian lei made of fragrant vines. "We just thought it was a lovely name for our daughter," Dawn Siemon said. "She was born in Hawaii and we felt it was right that the child and Hawaii should somehow be intertwined. The word means 'outpouring of love.' " Their first child, Jeff, was born there the year before.

Although he never claimed to eat the bones of fullbacks for brunch, Jeff Siemon became a Pro Bowl linebacker in 1973, and he repeated in 1975 and 1976. In that same twelve-month span he spent several weeks at a seminary in St. Paul studying theology, joined with friends to form a financial consulting group called Pro Financial Coordinators, traveled, prayed, made enough money from all pursuits to put him beyond $75,000 annually—and didn't strike any of his friends as changing Jeff Siemon in any essential way. He grieved over the release in early fall of his closest friend on the Vikings, Doug Kingsriter. And in the weeks that followed he expressed his support and loyalty with prayer, phone calls and personal visits, trying to root Doug onto another team.

It is not the kind of conduct the football fan will quickly associate with a 235-pound linebacker. If religion is not your program, you can call it gentleness. Or you can call it, as Siemon does, Christianity.

Siemon is wary about using the term extravagantly. He found himself feeling those reservations late in the 1976 season, in the playoff game with the Rams.

"When I came in off the bench and began playing in the second quarter, my old friend Rich Saul greeted me with something very nonchalant, like "Hi Jeff, how are you doin'?' Rich is one of the great centers in football. We've played against each other several times now, and we have been together a number of times at Christian-oriented activities. Still, it was an unusual and fine gesture in the midst of a pressure game like this. I nodded in return. Which is why I felt a little sheepish a few minutes later when I had to scream to an official, 'He's holding. He's holding.' Which he was. Although he is a great football player and a fine Christian, Rich happens to be one of the most accomplished holders among the NFL centers. So, believe it or not, I had to scream for justice."

It put God, Jeff conceded later, in a terrible predicament.

6

Once a year in the life of a professional football team there is a Philadelphia Week. It isn't usually called that; it doesn't normally have a title at all. But the ball player recognizes its symptoms instantly. Somber men are overtaken by giggles. The week's practice resembles some old Ed Norton script.

Approaching midseason, the Minnesota Vikings stood 5-0-1. They had won two games by only one point and were beginning to alarm their sympathizers, who wailed about the unscenic quality of the Viking victories. And they had just beaten the New York Giants 24–7 in a game which received an unsentimental evaluation from Alan Page.

"Personally, I thought the game was dull. It was one of those October Sundays when a man really should be walking in the leaves. I spent part of that last long drive on the bench watching the fans. It was educational." (Which simply established that the afternoon wasn't a complete loss for Page or the Vikings.)

Undefeated, the Vikings looked wistfully for somebody they could impress. Plainly they had not impressed their fans, who craved some truly barbaric onslaught by the Vikings. It was one thing to win—a lot of teams could do that—but to win and look awesome, that was big league stuff! Who needs tension?

For several weeks the Vikings' level of awesomeness had been extremely modest. They almost blew a long lead against the Bears, and they needed Nate Allen's near-spike to avoid plunging some of the fans into a deep trance. The national magazines ignored them in their preoccupation with such wonder teams as the Baltimore Colts, the New England Patriots, the Los Angeles Rams and the Dallas Cowboys. But when even Howard Cosell ignored the Vikings, their fans complained as though this should be classified as some kind of impoverishment.

Under these conditions the Vikings may have earned—even demanded—a Philadelphia Week. In the mind of the typical football freak, the days preceding an NFL game are fraught with granite-grim postures on the field and tense scholarship in the projection room.

From Jeff Siemon's journal

Tuesday, October 19   Chuck Foreman, who has been threatening to try for the movies, turned casting director today. He volunteered to find a part for Chuck Goodrum, our offensive guard, who has never announced any acting ambitions.

It happened after we finally made one of those gadget plays work, one where somebody unexpected throws the ball. For years the Vikings have been trying to find some presentable combination to use on the halfback pass that Paul Hornung used to run so well for Green Bay. We have tried it with Dave Osborn and Ed Marinaro. We even tried it a couple of times with Chuck Foreman. This time Sammy White out on the flank took one step forward, two backward, and caught the ball thrown by Tarkenton. Sammy then faked running. We use that little flanker screen all the time, but this time he lifted his arm and threw deep. It caught the defense completely unawares and the pass was completed.

When Charlie Goodrum saw Sammy throw that nice pass he said he was glad we finally found somebody who could throw the ball.

Foreman was within earshot, of course, and it was a clear slander of Foreman's pass throwing ability. "You know Goodrum," he said, "I think you could play in the movies. And I think I know what part suits you. Blackula [a movie starring a black Dracula]." The ball players howled. Foreman thought it was such a great line he volunteered to write Tarkenton's stuff for his Grandstand show.

Wednesday, October 20 The coaches unleashed James (Duck) White and Mark Mullaney on the pass rush again today, and they had the offense pretty well scrambled in short order. Duck especially is a terror in certain situations where he can pin his ears back and just fly. It's the most realistic training imaginable for our offensive line, but some of the people there have to believe nobody needs all that realism. Ed White is one. Ed is really one of the fine guards in football, definitely all pro. But when you turn loose a guy like Duck, sooner or later he's going to beat even the best blockers. He had Ed reeling again today. Duck got so realistic he unintentionally bumped into Bobby Lee and hurt Bobby's ankle, which is just about the one unforgivable sin of a pro football practice, hurting your own quarterback. None of the offense's misery was lost on Alan Page. "Duck," Alan announced in a make-believe lecture, "you've got a lot of nerve knocking football's strongest man on his can."

Ed White just glowered, which I'm sure is something he can lead the league in when he really tries. Nobody glowers as superbly as Ed White.

Thursday, October 21 Bud called everyone together as always, because this was Thursday, and said it appeared everybody was loose. We sort of smiled, agreeing. He said everybody appeared to be having a good time. We smiled some more. Then he said we'd better get serious because we had a ball game coming up.

Nobody smiled anymore.

Not for the record, anyhow.

Friday, October 22 Paul Krause, our free safety, who has never claimed to be the most ferocious tackler in the NFL, counterattacked today. We were running plays inside the 15-yard line, and there isn't supposed to be a whole lot of contact. But on this play Stu Voigt, the rugged and powerful tight end, came across with Krause covering. Stu caught the pass and Krause just decked him.

I saw the play out of the corner of my eye, and as I came over, without looking at the defensive player, I said, "nice play, Wally." I thought it was Wally because Hilgenberg has both the disposition and wallop to deliver that blow to a tough guy like Stu Voigt. I nearly gasped when I saw it was Paul. There were also some coos of amazement from around the field. Nobody had a harder time adjusting to it than Stu Voigt.

I joined the rest of the defense in giving Stu the best jibes we could think of, loaded with originality and bile.

We finally got our record player and tape recorder set up in the locker room, and we are getting ear-blasting concerts all the time now. This is the outfit our equipment manager, Stubby Eason, installed on his own after a couple of the players were unable to raise enough cash. Stubby is one of those beautiful combinations of hard-boiled politician and good-natured tyrant. He's completely trusted by the guys, but everybody gets on him unmercifully if he doesn't deliver all the haberdashery in the locker room when they need it. Eason is a terrific counterpuncher, though, and he gives better than he gets.

Anyhow, he set up this tape recorder. Since it's more popular by far with the black players than the white, it's playing black music about 100 percent of the time. Not all the people who dig that kind of music in our locker room are black, of course, and not everybody who has doubts is white. Marshall, Winston, Hilgenberg and I were pretending to engineer a timetable for using it today. Jim Marshall, who is black, said the fairest solution was an equal time setup. White players would play their music from 10:30 to 11:30, he said, and black players from 11:30 to 12:30.

Practice starts at 12:30. Most players get to the stadium between 11:30 and noon, which means that the place would be deserted for the whites' appointed concert hour.

To implement the Marshall Plan in the afternoon, he said, blacks could listen to the tape recorder from the end of practice to 4 P.M., and whites from 5 to 5:30.

Most of the players are long gone by 5 P.M.

We told Jim there was no way the Marshall Plan was going to be ratified. He just smiled because it already had been. Everything on the tape recorder is soul music.

Sunday, October 24   Game day in Philadelphia, where it was drizzling and gloomy and the pavements got splashed when traffic went by. I try to be orderly and methodical the morning of games. Today at chapel we had a black preacher who worked in downtown Philadelphia. He did a good job and the meeting was reasonably well attended.

As part of being well organized on game mornings, I like to be down in the hotel lobby with a few minutes to spare. Bud's buses always leave on time—which on this day was 11:50 A.M.—and it's an automatic $100 fine if you miss. I was lying on my bed at about 11:35, wearing trousers and no shirt and thinking about putting my gear together, when Fred Cox walked in. It happens that the deodorant can I use is too large for my toiletries bag, so I have gotten into the habit of borrowing Fred's deodorant. This time I noticed his deodorant can was missing. While he was still in the room I walked next door to borrow Jeff Wright's. He wasn't there, so I walked into another room to borrow some from Bob Lee. He and his roommate were ready to go, but he opened his bag for me and gave me his deodorant, which I used.

As I walked back to my room I remembered leaving the chain in the door so it wouldn't lock and leaving my key on the dresser. Just as I walked out of Lee's room I saw Cox about to turn the corner. I yelled, "Fred, do you have the key?"

He said he left it in the room—which of course was locked.

My watch read 11:45.

Cox shouted down the hall to say he was going for another key, and with that he entered the elevator, which seemed to be carrying the whole Viking offense plus a half dozen delegates to a carpenter's convention.

Minutes ticked by. I was standing in the Philadelphia Hilton without a shirt, locked out of my room, and it was two minutes from bus departure time. Jeff Siemon, the man always in control! People were staring at this half-naked oaf. I got behind a pillar and just stood there, feeling miserable and sorry for myself. Cox finally showed with a minute to go. I ran into the room, got my stuff and flew into the elevator, whose doors were just closing.

I reached the second bus just as the first one—bearing Grant—was pulling out. If we ever win this football game, I told myself, somebody higher than me is going to get most of the credit.

For a long time not even a higher power appeared willing to claim credit. Against great odds the Vikings once more managed to create suspense. It is not easy for an undefeated football team to trail the Philadelphia Eagles, 9–0, with less than a minute left in the half, but the Vikings did it with a remarkable show of versatility. Chuck Foreman fumbled a handoff into an eventual Eagle field goal. Francis Tarkenton threw for an interception that later produced an Eagle touchdown. Neil Clabo shanked a punt. Duck White, possibly mistaking the Philadelphia punter for teammate Ed White, ran into the innocent Eagle to further complicate life for the hugely favored Vikings. At this moment Siemon's faux pas at the hotel seemed to be catching: Everybody on the team appeared to be dually occupied trying to protect his decency and groping for the key.

Novel methods were demanded to rescue the team from the lingering lethargy of a slaphappy week. Stern poses were out of the question. Who would believe them? Into the void rode two mischievous gamins from the briar patch, Francis Tarkenton and Chuck Foreman.

The disciplines of rehearsed football, such as diagrammed plays and programmed maneuvers, have never dominated either of them. Tarkenton became a millionaire by carefully avoiding rehearsed football. Foreman can never recount or explain his moves; he has always run intuitively, with unpredictable spins and pivots that cannot be engineered or sometimes even controlled. But something about the patriotic environment of Philadelphia, or perhaps the Eagle defense, stirred both of them to new frontiers of independent thought and deed. It was about what would have happened if the Katzenjammer kids had been given $400,000 and a football. They improvised on the run, manufactured plays in the huddle and cued each other with hand signals. Before it was over Foreman was wheezing for air, his 200 yards on the ground safely stashed in the team record books. Tarkenton was safely past 40,000 passing yards for his career, and Grant was hastily trying to figure out how he was going to diagram all of this turnip-field football on his television show the next day.

With the Vikings lurching along, 17–12, in the fourth quarter, Tarkenton handed the ball to Brent McClanahan diving into the line. The handoff executed, Tarkenton carried out a fake option run down the line of scrimmage with Foreman trailing. Six people mauled McClanahan; everybody ignored Foreman.

"Did you see it?" Foreman asked Tarkenton walking back to the huddle.

"I had big eyes for it," Tarkenton said. "We got to wait. We can't run that again until first down when they're in the same defense." From the Philadelphia 32 on first down, two plays later, Tarkenton faked to McClanahan diving into the line.

Six people mauled McClanahan.

Since the other five were occupied on the opposite side of the field, pure mathematics decreed that nobody could take any interest in Foreman—except, of course, for Tarkenton, who still had the ball, which he lateraled to the unguarded fullback. He could have run all day if the goal line hadn't intervened after 32 yards. Everyone in purple howled spontaneously—save for McClanahan, who was securely interred in the artificial turf beneath six plucked Eagles.

Having resisted stoutly until then, the Eagles surprisingly conceded with eight minutes to play by punting the ball from the Viking 36 while trailing, 24–12. Grant concluded there was no ethical reason why Chuck Foreman should not be allowed a few extra plays to establish a new Viking ground record. It was no display of misty sentiment. Running backs tend to acquire bonus money and salary on the basis of such statistics. And since Foreman and the Viking management were going to be embroiled in accountants' ledgers for months to come, a coach doesn't remove the employee on the brink of some dividends if he values the employee's loyalty. Tarkenton, informed of the situation, called a play. "If you see me put my hand on my helmet," Tarkenton told Foreman, "we're changing the play."

Bill Cosby could not have produced it more lovingly.

Tarkenton saw the Eagles' overshift, and so did the offensive line, but Foreman crouching behind them couldn't. Tarkenton didn't want to betray the new call he was going to make. The offensive line automatically allowed for it when the defense shifted. Tarkenton tapped his helmet. Foreman recognized the cue, rammed behind Ed White and Ron Yary and charged 46 yards to his record.

"I would have scratched the new play on the ground in the huddle," Tarkenton said later, "the way we used to back in fifth grade. But how do you scratch a play into artificial turf?"

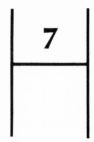

7

An editor of a national magazine, in the omni-minded style of
national magazine editors, queried a Minneapolis correspon-
dent about Francis Tarkenton as the 1976 football season
lengthened. Such communiques rarely take the uninspired
form of simple, direct questions; they must be preceded by the
editor's Working Hypothesis, which is frequently of a length
that outdistances that of the projected study itself. This is followed by an encyclopedic outpouring of questions, spur-of-the-
moment insights and, finally, historical background. Tarkenton
of course was deemed worthy of the full arsenal of editorial
bravura.

Consider, the editor said: Here was Francis Tarkenton, once
a laughing, seraph-eyed choir boy of a quarterback, happily
married to the princess of his dreams, a campus beauty. Francis
Tarkenton had been uncannily healthy for sixteen years. His
durability was almost a proverb in football. Because of it he had
harvested every major passing record in pro history, accomplished with a scampering style totally alien to the pros' (and
the fans') concept of classic quarterbacking. But his records, his
masterful grasp of the game and the excitement he had gener-

ated combined with his restless capitalism to make Francis Tarkenton a millionaire.

Yet in 1976, the scenario continued—dissonant French horns were almost audible offstage here—the idyll was threatened. The hero's plantation was growing thorns and some vagrant weeds. He was separated from his wife. For the first time in sixteen years he had failed to start a game because of injury. There were rumors that the head coach had benched him in one game, rumors that persisted despite clenched-teeth denials by Tarkenton and his coach. He wasn't throwing as many touchdown passes as he did in 1975, and there were reports about his weakened arm. Also, he looked longer of tooth and thinner of hair.

Surely, it was surmised, this must be the most troubled of years for Francis Tarkenton, one of the country's most celebrated athletes, whose career was still hounded by his failure to Win the Big One.

Would the troubled Francis Tarkenton care to respond?

"Yes," he said. "I'm moved that people should be concerned what kind of year I think 1976 is."

"And what kind of year is it?"

"I think it's been colossal."

Are there any other questions?

Francis Tarkenton was being Francis Tarkenton—the unexpurgated version. Life's excitements and rewards are bounded only by the limits of one's curiosities and energies, he was saying. It has setbacks, yes; a bust in the ribs from Paul Naumoff is a setback. A marital problem could be jarring, but it was, after all, nobody's business but that of the family. The prattling by Jimmy the Greek about an imaginary friction between the quarterback and the coach can be infuriating. So call the Greek a petty gossip and a discredit to the network that airs him. Winning The Big One bothers writers and fans more than it bothers the man who allegedly can't win it. And with a team heading for the playoffs and possibly the Super Bowl, why should a man who holds all the passing records worry about touchdown passes? That was a game he might have played ten years ago.

He reaffirmed the basic dilemma of Francis Tarkenton, the man for all environments and any third-and-long situation you could imagine. His trouble was not having time to do everything he knew he could do. And his appetites were still intensifying in 1976. Before millions of fascinated gazers each weekend, he now literally led two lives as a creature of television: He was both performing artist and critic, practitioner and philosopher. As a quarterback he wore the conventional football armory and subjected himself to the dual risk of dismemberment by enemy tackles and the scrutiny of his television colleagues. But after the brawling he would be on view in headset and intelligent forehead, spreading his erudition for the same audience that thirty minutes before had gaped at him as a scurrying jock.

His mobility was matched by that of the NBC architects who built a $25,000 transmission tower near his suburban Minneapolis home to air his Minnesota-based expertise and raised a similar apparatus near his off-season home in Atlanta.

Football scarcely intruded on his diversified industries, which included a behavior management service in Atlanta, investments, real estate and promotional work. He ran them in hours-long telephone sessions from the Viking training room after practices, from a rented office in the Viking headquarters and on off-day flights to New York and Atlanta. On the surface his schedule looked frantic, and in operation it looked about the same. Still, he was unfailingly ready each football practice—and supremely ready each Sunday afternoon.

Tarkenton literally could not get enough of life and the exhilarations that wait to be discovered or created. What he missed in his earlier reach for competitive success and multisided fulfillment he sought later in a headlong rush for a new identity. And if he did experience problems, it was in choosing what identity he should occupy this hour. Should it be Francis

94

the superstar, Francis the entrepreneur, Francis the with-it free expressionist, Francis the thoughtful, Francis the globetrotter or Francis the television guru?

That he could somehow harmonize these identities most of the time or focus the appropriate one at the right time was a gauge of his self-possession and his acrobatic psyche.

In his sixteenth year of pro football, he was on a continuing high. If the football business and the entertainment business were inseparable, he had got everything together in 1976 as a national star at the highest level of visibility. As a football wiseman the audiences found him increasingly saucy at times, blunt and then engaging, testy and charming. He was impatient with some of the fans' and the players' old conceptions and anxious for the world to adopt Fran Tarkenton's own. He went to work each day with his mind whirling in a clutter that appeared impossible to organize: telephone interviews, tapes, business calls, correspondence. But at 11 A.M. he shunted it all aside and opened the door to his locker at the stadium.

The complexities of his life translated into millions of dollars and a show biz aura—and later the ultimate public recognition: gossip and curiosity about his private life. But he never revealed evidence of stress in the locker room or in the huddle, and certainly never on the line of scrimmage.

Not many years before, his statements to reporters were informative but careful. Sometimes he sounded like a pixie and sometimes like a college professor. After sixteen years, with his credibility as a quarterback and a civilized man of his times established, he felt free to sound outrageous and, at times, to act that way.

"A quarterback has to let all of the speculative manure surrounding a ball game slide into the drain," he said. "The quarterback gets booed, idolized, hung in effigy, written about, and sometimes gossiped about. All that. And then he has to slam it all back."

He was not talking about a quarterback retaliating with a

dazzling performance on Sunday. He was talking about the quarterback getting up each morning to confront the rising sun in the Tarkenton style.

One of his personal outlets was buffoonery and mock harangues in the locker room. He would not have indulged in that years ago, before time had given him status and before his performance had given him the trust of his teammates. He has a roughened, noisy language behind the dressing room door now, and he affects the old pro role with tobacco in his jaw. But most of that is style rather than substance; it is the rushing celebrity's safety valve. What he still did best in 1976, better than practically anybody in football, was to think, gamble, strive and lead.

There was little resentment of him among his teammates. A lot of envy, yes. But he had paid his dues; he had delivered for sixteen years. When he was in a huddle there was nothing in the football game that shook him or threatened him. His belief in his ability to find a way was unconditional.

He didn't always deliver; now and then his ego or his impetuosity cost the team. When he failed it was not usually because he guessed wrong but because his tired arm was inadequate to the gall of his decision. But he was too smart to make unreasonable demands on his arm very often, and so his best passes week in and week out were his lobs to his great running back, Foreman, or his still-crisp 15-yarders to the curling and slanting wide receivers. His deep passes had the rainbow's curvature, but they were always low-risk maneuvers. Because of the defensive alignments they were thrown against, many of them reached friendly hands.

The alleged benching in Detroit began as an honest (and natural) misinterpretation by a network announcer of Grant's sideline remarks. It graduated into a weekly washline special for Jimmy the Greek, a likeable promoter and huckster who poses as a football expert. Although CBS takes care to disassociate his gossip from the so-called gambling line, it is actually peddling Jimmy as a tout to millions of people who are smitten by Las Vegas characters. His reputation from the beginning was piggybacked on that of a genuine Nevada gambler named Nick the Greek. Jimmy now knows the NFL reasonably well, though not as well as the matron's delight who acts as his straight man on the Greek's interludes, Brent Musberger. The Greek in any case had plenty of time to overtake the truth of the Detroit incident. He told his audiences in all seriousness, however, about the imaginary split between Tarkenton and Grant, who have never had an uncomplimentary thing to say about each other in five years.

What did the viewers in Walla Walla know about torn ribs or about five years of mutual respect between player and coach? For that matter, what did the Greek know? (as the Greek himself explained later). Tarkenton, after all, looked so glum on the sidelines he *must* have been teed off at the coach.

So Tarkenton went on TV with Howard Cosell to denounce the Greek. It was not a bad triangle. On CBS the Greek snipes at NBC's Francis Tarkenton, whereupon Tarkenton grabs an ABC microphone to blister the Greek. The only absentees from the libretto were Norman Van Brocklin and PBC.

From there it escalated. If the Greek is going to start shooting at quarterbacks, Tarkenton snorted, he should have picked somebody who doesn't know the business. Snyder accused Tarkenton of being vindictive. Hearing that, Tarkenton nearly fainted from hysterics. The Greek, he said, had impugned Tarkenton's relationship with his coach in front of millions of people; and now he was crying when Tarkenton retaliated.

"What does he want," Tarkenton asked, "a valentine?"

Later in the year CBS routinely asked Tarkenton to appear on a post-game show. It might have had reservations about that, owing to the Tarkenton-Greek embroilment, but you can't very well ignore a man who throws three touchdown passes. Tarkenton had no corporate quarrel with CBS and in the past had been Mr. Conviviality on camera with the network's other happy faces. But when the producer dispatched his courier to the dressing room, Tarkenton told the courier to stick the invitation in his zoom lens.

"Any network that gives a forum to somebody like Jimmy the Greek doesn't deserve consideration," he said. "I can't control anybody or anything except me. And I'm not going to do it, for exactly that reason."

The Greek, to the astonishment of nobody, was back on CBS the next Sunday gossiping effortlessly and spotting the San Francisco 49ers the conventional two points for knowing the seagulls' bombardment pattern at Candlestick Park.

To Jeff Siemon, Francis Tarkenton had been an absorbing personality study from their first meeting. For awhile a part of the churchgoing public tended to link them as Christian brothers wearing the same uniform. Francis, the son of a Methodist preacher, was quickly established in the public mind as a football-playing hymn singer. He addressed hundreds of prayer meetings and in 1968 authored a testament to the life of a believer in the huddles of big-time football. In later years his growing sophistication altered both his lifestyle and his expression of the religious ethic. He moved away from the gospel meeting flavor of his early involvement and thought of religion more in terms of human sensitivity and the conversion of God-given talents and energies to uses that could benefit people less favored.

The more fundamental believers who had ardently greeted him as a champion of the faith years earlier said they were puzzled by Francis Tarkenton's changes.

Francis Tarkenton said a man must be truthful to himself and the kind of faith that is meaningful to him.

Jeff Siemon, a Christian by the conventional definition, made no judgment of Francis Tarkenton as a Christian. Francis sometimes attended Viking chapel service. But on the days they shared the training room facilities as members of Fred Zamberletti's casualty corps, they usually talked football, politics, economics, group psychology—whatever struck a chord of mutual interest to two inquisitive and opinionated minds. Siemon welcomed those sessions. The two seemed to stimulate each other, and he found himself listening in amused admiration as Tarkenton delivered one thunderclap opinion after another, ranging from their strategy against the Lion defense to the state of politics in Georgia. There was a ceaseless vibrancy to this quarterback-capitalist-philosopher-authority about town. He met the world head-on with total confidence and swashbuckling eagerness, and if sometimes he was wrong-headed or beaten, tomorrow he could set it right. Or on the next play. Or on the next telephone call.

If tuning in on the private lives of their troubled heroes is a windfall for the superstar galleries, Tarkenton allowed no such bonus. A football player's private life, he said, was his own, and he doesn't have to yield to the public's curiosity. He made only a minimal statement at the time of his separation. "If people wish to talk about it there's nothing I can do to control that, and nothing I care to," he said. "I'm comfortable with myself, and with those who matter to me."

With all of the records behind him, Tarkenton had no infatuation with the statistics in 1976. By his standards they were ordinary. The Viking offense was uneven, although this was not necessarily a reflection of the quarterback's performance. The emergence of Sammy White and Ahmad Rashad as one of the ranking wide receiver combinations in football, along with Chuck Foreman's unequaled versatility in the backfield, gave Tarkenton all the instruments he needed for the kind of passing offensive he handled best, with plenty of options and spontaneity. Foreman was going to get his thousand yards on the ground again, but the Vikings' running game suffered from a certain lack of charisma. This didn't hurt it quite as much as the absence of a mauling fullback and the flareups of mediocrity up front.

Tarkenton usually managed to find a way, though, if by doing nothing more than nurturing the lead and avoiding blunders on days when the defense dominated or Matt Blair or Alan Page or Nate Allen was blocking somebody's kick. In the sixteenth year of his stewardship in the NFL huddles, he could now win some football games on the raw force of his leadership—which his old detractors had claimed he would never be able to do.

His old detractors should have been required to witness the Minnesota Vikings play the Detroit Lions on November 7 at Metropolitan Stadium. And not only the game, perhaps, but the days preceding it, because this was a week and a game that rang with all the Tarkenton rhythms of football as he perceived it: a struggle of mind and nerve, a forum for both the impulsive act and hard-jowled professionalism and a happy hours shootout where nobody gets killed and 50 million people get entertained.

And Sir Francis, the Aging Galahad, wins.

They had absorbed their first loss of the season, 14–13, to the Bears and Walter Payton, but the playoffs were still secure, and nobody but the Minnesota fan was disposed to grieve for the future of Viking football. It was one of those weeks of decision, however. The Viking offense was having an ordinary season, and so was Francis Tarkenton. And they were facing a Lion defense that historically had disrupted Tarkenton's game plans and sometimes his ribs.

The primary architect of these encroachments was James (Gummy) Carr, one of pro football's more popular coaching gypsies, a chatty character with a head full of country phrases and a drawing board full of blitzers. Nobody in the NFL played defense quite the way Gummy Carr did. Other teams played four-threes and odd-mans and three-man lines. No one has figured out a designation for Gummy's defense. On the diagram charts it looks like a prison break. Everybody is going over the wall. Sometimes Gummy blitzes one linebacker, sometimes two, sometimes three. Sometimes he also blitzes a safetyman and sometimes two. An NFL quarterback can count on looking into a *nine-man* blitz three or four times a game when he faces

Detroit—assuming he was still vertical enough to count the last one.

As a defensive coordinator Gummy wins some games with those tactics and loses some. He might average about the same with conventional defenses. But his blitzes, slants, loops and gang attacks have the virtue of making life equally suspenseful and therefore miserable for (a) the Lions' opponent and (b) the Lions. Neither has the faintest idea how they are going to turn out.

Tarkenton in the week of the Lions decided not to be miserable. With the approval of Jerry Burns, the offensive coordinator, Francis decided the Vikings would look Gummy Carr's blitzers straight in the eye and shoot for a touchdown every time they rushed. And they would not do it with the little gumball lobs to Chuck Foreman or sideline screens that sometimes embarrass a rushing defense.

Every time the Lions showed a blitz, Tarkenton was going to throw deep—or at least every time he was still upright. Maybe Tarkenton decided the taunts about the Vikings' dump-it-off offense were getting thick. Or maybe he liked a good staring contest. On the other hand, maybe the bomb was the best way to beat Gummy's wildman defense.

A quarterback could bring it off if he could stand up to the storming herd because he had seen it so many times; if he knew when the blitzers were serious and when they were pretending to blitz; and if he knew when to switch the play on the line of scrimmage and he could enlist uninhibited creatures on his team who liked to play the same game.

Francis Tarkenton knew such a quarterback.

"They can't beat us if they blitz us," he told the Vikings all week. "If they want to play chicken with us in front of the whole country, we'll play. If they give us the defense of the 1960s, we'll give them the long bombs of the 1960s."

Seldom has the football counterpart of Russian roulette been played so unabashedly, or before a wider audience than the national television crowd that augmented the 48,000 gazers at moonlit Metropolitan Stadium. For four days he had been pumping up the Viking offense, selling his renovated passing game. Gummy Carr was going to send everybody but Chief Pontiac. Let him. He, Francis, would go for the end zone. If Gummy blitzed, Tarkenton would hold in Foreman and McClanahan to block. This would launch Sammy and Ahmad Rashad one-on-one against Lem Barney and Levi Johnson.

Every football coach in the audience must have salivated at the sight, because it was football right off the clinic wall. Gummy's blitzers against the trigger mind of a thirty-six-year-old quarterback who had seen it all.

Neither side backed off from their pre-game strategy. Leading or trailing, early or late, the Lions rushed their linebackers and sometimes their safeties. They made no concessions to Tarkenton's sixteen years of battle ribbons. They had the No. 1 defense in the NFL and they weren't going to change its bumptious personality or its stampeding behavior. Accepting the arrangement, the Vikings themselves were predicting before the game that the Lions were either going to be bombed back to the ice age or Tarkenton would be plastered to the goal posts.

The issue was joined on the opening series. The Lions charged with seven men and Tarkenton threw 55 yards to Sammy White. The ball missed by five inches. A couple of minutes later he hit one almost as deep. It was going to be a game of long ball in the wind and the gloaming, an internal game.

"It couldn't have happened," he said after he had thrown for 347 yards and the Vikings had won, 31–23, "without the game of the year from our offensive line, Yary, White, Goodrum, Tingelhoff, Riley and Voigt, and the backs hanging in there to pick up the blitzers."

Yet with less than two minutes remaining young Sammy White on the flank had suffered the torment of a schoolboy who, in his eagerness to show off his new suit, had lost his pants.

There were 50 million witnesses to his social blunder. It would not have been especially repugnant to Sammy if it were nothing more awkward than losing his trousers in public. He hadn't done that—they were secure. It was the ball game that was in jeopardy, and Sammy White was the young man wearing the horns.

A few minutes before, Sammy White had captured one of Tarkenton's passes as he hurtled toward the end zone. He was yards behind the defensive back, Levi Johnson, and his heart was a skyrocket. As the goal line appeared three strides ahead of him, Sammy lifted his arm to announce to the world with all the exultation erupting inside of him that on November 7, 1976, he, Sammy White, was scoring his second touchdown of the day against the Detroit Lions and wasn't it all just so fantastic and beautiful?

"I felt so good," he said later, "I wanted to dance and sing. We were ahead and I knew I was about to score to clinch the game, so I just held the ball up. I wasn't going to spike it. The coach says that's showboating. And he's right. I don't know what holding the ball over your head is, but whatever it is I'm never gonna do it again because I felt this tug on my shoe, and there I went, and there went the ball into the end zone. I saw a guy fall on it, and it was the wrong uniform. I never felt so terrible and miserable."

The uniform and the football belonged to a grinning Levi Johnson. The tug on Sammy's shoe was inflicted by the Lions' other cornerback, Lem Barney, who had raced crossfield and overtaken Sammy White just as he slowed up to display his trophy to an admiring world.

Barney made hash out of the ceremonies.

Sammy tripped before he reached the goal line and lost the ball before he got into the end zone. It was ruled a touchback.

His route back to the Viking bench steered Sammy unavoidably within the view of Harry P. Grant. It was one of the longest and saddest miles in the anthologies of human remorse. White feared immediate deportation. Instead Grant spoke briefly. "There's a difference between show biz and show boat," he said. "What you did was show boat. It cost us a touchdown. A player can be happy and show it, but don't be happy by doing something stupid. You'll get another chance."

Sammy White, penitent receiver, squirmed in his three-point stance across the line of scrimmage from Levi Johnson with less than two minutes on the scoreboard. He was talking to himself. It wouldn't have done any good to talk to Johnson. Cornerbacks are notoriously unsympathetic to suffering receivers.

"Please throw me the ball, Francis," Sammy said, "just once more."

There are times when a man, twenty-two and in deep trouble, can't wait for the slow-grinding wheels of redemption. Could he have imagined it a year ago at Grambling College, not far from where he grew up in the swamp country? He was a fellow with a happy soul and restless feet, but he never thought he would be catching all those passes from the one and only Francis Tarkenton before millions of people just a few months later. But Lord, what had he done? Made himself a fool, dropping the ball like that. And here it was, the temperature below freezing, the night wind blowing in his face, and he told himself, "Mamma, they better throw me the ball on this next play because I got troubles."

His list of people who deserved some immediate atonement began with Harry P. Grant and moved methodically through 46,735 people in the grandstand, his mother and father in Monroe, Louisiana, his girlfriend in the stands. The roster had no limits.

He glanced down the line at the quarterback chanting his cadence. If anybody could bail him out, Sammy determined, Francis Tarkenton could. Francis was his patron, his counselor and his refuge. These kindnesses Sammy repaid by catching Francis' passes with great productivity. In Francis' mind this always enhanced the fine personal virtues of any fellow human being, especially a rookie.

The Lions blitzed their linebackers again. Sammy approved with a bolt of hope. It meant that one more time he would race man-on-man against Levi Johnson. He gave Johnson a shoulder

104

and hip and then sprinted diagonally toward the goal posts. The Lions' blitzers raged to no avail against Tarkenton's bodyguards. Francis lofted the ball deep. Like a delinquent waif seizing the bonbon of forgiveness, Sammy clutched the ball and loped into the end zone to complete a 37-yard touchdown pass, the seventh pass he had caught in the game for a Viking record of 210 yards.

He did not hold the ball over his head. He did not fling the ball onto the frozen dead grass. He did not hula in the end zone in the manner of that stud fullback from the Lions, Lawrence Gaines. What he did was to carry the ball with two hands *through* the end zone. If they had wanted, he would have carried the ball with two hands into the next time zone. When the officials came for the ball they were nearly forced to pry it away.

On the sidelines he felt Francis Tarkenton hug him, and he was speechless to think he and this great quarterback were teammates. How could there be a bigger day than this? He couldn't understand everything Tarkenton was saying and laughing about, but it must be okay. And then, back in the dressing room, here was this famous millionaire quarterback clearing away chairs. What was the man up to? He was mugging and screaming and he said Sammy, I'll tell you how it was. Faithfully he reproduced Sammy's epic scene, the ball overhead, the stumble on the goal line. The ball splattered against the locker room wall and Francis Tarkenton shagged after it on his hands and knees.

More than forty alleged football robots howled and applauded and sang a song for Sammy White before presenting him with the game ball.

A few hours later the born-again rookie receiver of the Minnesota Vikings telephoned his parents in Louisiana.

"Son," his mother asked, "did you learn anything today?"

He explained what he had learned.

"Son," his father asked, "do you mind telling your father what in hell you were doing?"

He had less success explaining that.

But he had no trouble explaining the kind of football player Francis Tarkenton was to a young fellow out of the swamp country of Louisiana.

In the sixteenth year of his professional football career, Francis Tarkenton acknowledged that not everybody saw him the way Sammy White did. Some saw him as self-indulgent, a pleasure-seeker in his athletic maturity, coarser in his language and franker in his appetites. Others saw him as a man unable to find enough hours in the day to capitalize himself and to feed his curiosities and his ambitions. His closest friends saw him as a man who lived faster and harder, but who was still what he had been sixteen years before: a vibrant human being who, although he fought for and expanded his place in the universe, still recognized the sensibilities of others and the need for faith in them, and a faith in something higher that directed his life and others'.

One judgment of Tarkenton hadn't changed. If you blitz him, the Lions said, you better be ready.

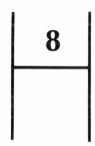

8

When forty-three athlete prodigies pledge their fortunes and the welfare of their ribcages to each other every day for five months, they assume certain house privileges. Among these is the right to scrutinize each other's behavior and their Dun & Bradstreet ratings.

The right is inspired both by normal nosiness and the imperatives of the trade. A man puts his shoulders next to yours on the goal line: Together you might make thousands of dollars and achieve some higher communion, or you might blow it all by getting wiped out on a trap play. Ball players are like anybody else. It makes life a little more significant and a lot juicier when they understand themselves better.

To relieve the tensions of their business and the demands of their individuality in a team environment, they tease each other's pretensions and expose their vulnerabilities. It is a game conducted by skilled fencers; sometimes it is the most hilarious comedy in town.

They hone the arts of the mimic and lampooner because these are a defense and comfort against the tyrannies of the scoreboard and the waiver list. They experience far more attention than most human beings, and in many cases they are awarded unwarranted importance. But on the other side of the scale is the frailness of their fame and the line they must walk every week—sometimes every play—between the public's acclaim and its derision.

Their professional lives, and sometimes their private lives, are a succession of verdicts: the verdict of the coach at cutdown time, the verdict of the score, the verdict of the paymaster and their own verdict when it's all over. They are paid better than bankers, but, perhaps for this reason, most of them are hounded harder by insecurity. The social conditions are unique; their closest buddies covet their job. The best of them achieve treasure and fame that might be envied by princes. But it flows from a fragile wellspring that can be choked off irretrievably by the tearing of a muscle.

So their glory, and that of their friends, is a very dicey thing. Because it is, they sometimes shrink from too heavy an emotional involvement with the pain and disability around them on the field. It is part of the occupation, and it has to be accepted.

From Jeff Siemon's journal

Tuesday, October 19   Scott Anderson, the young reserve offensive lineman who has had so much trouble trying to make it in the NFL the past couple of years, got hurt in practice today. We were going through a blitz drill in full pads at the time. Sometimes we run those drills close to full speed, which means you're exposed to injury. I blitzed the 5-hole between the offensive guard and tackle. Scott moved to pick me up. I hit into him and bounced outside. Matt Blair, the outside linebacker, was also blitzing, and a bunch of people just ran together. Scott got hit off balance and his knee buckled. You could tell immediately he was badly hurt. It was a shame to see it happen; he had just come back from a knee injury about a week earlier.

The scene was grotesque. Scott was down on the ground and tried to get up a second time. He couldn't, and he tried again. He pounded the ground in anger and hopelessness, knowing he probably faced an operation. The doctor confirmed it the next day.

Scott played at Missouri and is a player not many of the fans know. As a matter of fact some of the veteran players don't know him very well, either, because he has been on and off the team for a couple of years. He quit the squad a year ago but got another chance because the offensive line needed some depth and Scott can play either center or guard.

I hate to say it this way, but a kind of unwritten jungle law takes over at times like this. While you feel sadness anytime a ball player gets hurt, there is a fatalism in how the squad reacts. The axiom is "better he than me." So the next day it's as though a fellow like Scott was never there. They may like him, and certainly they sympathize with him. But not much time is spent worrying about him. He was there every day; now he's gone. Life goes on as though he were never there.

Another unwritten rule is that you'd better not get hurt if you value your position. Nate Allen had been hobbling most of the week. Nate is one of those who has a tendency to acquire nuisance injuries that leave him limping around. Several times today he was beaten deep on pass plays. In one sequence it happened four straight times. Finally Bud came over to the defensive huddle and said to Neill Armstrong, "Look, if he can't go, then I want someone else in there who can cover." With that they pulled Nate and put Bobby Bryant in.

Nobody had to stand on a podium and point out that this was the same Nate Allen who had played sensationally for the Vikings the first month. He saved us from a loss to the Rams and a tie with Detroit, and he knocked down three long bombs against New Orleans and intercepted two passes by the Steelers. But the third unwritten rule is: What can you do for us this week?

Bud Grant didn't invent it. It comes with the game. A player can feel resentful, but the bottom line is who will do the best job this week, not who deserves the gratitude.

Wally Hilgenberg never asked a coaching staff for gratitude and never asked an opponent for courtesy. As much as any player on the team, or in the league, his attitude and conduct as a pro football player was a reachback to the medieval years of the game. He was once reviled around the league as a head-hunter and a cheapshot, a man who played with open-handed malice and an instinct for the artery. In later years he reformed. Opponents and some friends maintained that his rehabilitation resulted more from Bud Grant's ultimatums than from any real contrition. You can be a tough guy, Grant conceded, but don't draw any more 15-yard penalties because nobody looks very tough sitting on the bench.

Hilgenberg decided to compromise. It was possible to be tough without being illegal. He settled (at least Charlie Sanders contended) for being merely obnoxious. But he also became a very competent linebacker who still played with the kind of heat the Vikings sorely needed in the years when they were said to ride to the ball park in refrigerated vans. Away from the field he was a personable fellow who allowed himself the line-backer's privilege—certain middle linebackers excepted—of being moody and occasionally rude. He and Siemon usually got along well, one playing off the other, because they were per-sonalities of glaring contrasts. Among the things Siemon and others found engrossing about Wally Hilgenberg were his stub-born little campaigns to sandbag people he thought were trying to move him out of the lineup.

From Jeff Siemon's journal

Wednesday, October 20　I fell in beside Wally on the walk down the stadium corridor to the film room. Wally is recovering from a charleyhorse, a deep thigh bruise. It seemed pretty bad right after last week's game, and he had it treated the next day. As he was walking to the film room he was sort of bounding around, and I said in mock surprise, "Wally, you mean you're going out today?"

He said, "I got it all figured out." He explained how he had adopted a timetable. He was going to nurse the injury for a day or two so he wouldn't have to risk the ailing thigh to practice. He pulled me aside. "I've got it figured out," he said. "They're so anxious to give my job away that I'm not going to let them. I'm going out there when I have to, and I'm going to surprise them all."

He was referring to an incident in the previous game when Neill Armstrong took him out with the explanation that Wally wasn't tackling well. This naturally had offended Wally. It wasn't hostility against the coach; he didn't want anybody on the team getting the idea he couldn't do the job, so he was letting the players know he was upset. Insecurity. We all have it.

A couple of days ago I was a guest at Bud Grant's weekly press luncheon, and he went out of his way to commend me for the job I was doing with the Viking kicking teams. Bud often uses the luncheons as a forum to commend his players publicly in ways he knows they will appreciate. I've had a couple of ordinary games, and he knew I was ready for some bucking up. I didn't think I would see the time I yearned for good words about how I was doing on the special teams. But I did. It really meant something.

How precarious the ball player's status is in his own eyes. Reinforcement, the psychologists call it. Everybody needs it in this business, crowded as it is with so many egos. I need it as much as the next guy, and probably more than some.

The fan may snicker at that. The ball player wouldn't. The ball player understands perfectly. He's like a professional speaker or a veteran tap dancer; no matter how many times you do it, you still want to be told you're doing it right. Another person who might understand is the kid who spells a tough word right in third grade. So when you say professionals, and when you use the expression "cool professionalism," you might remember Wally and Jeff Siemon.

The emergence of Ahmad Rashad as a star receiver and game-breaker to match Sammy White on the other side was an unforeseen bonus for the Viking offense. It also foreshadowed the departure of Jim Lash, who for several years had played dependably if almost anonymously on the Viking flank. Jim was a quiet man with sound mechanical attributes and competitive qualities. But he was never going to be a deep touchdown threat, and it was doubtful that he would uncover that key to the money chests for the wide receiver, the ability to make the critical play consistently.

In late October the San Francisco 49ers cast around for a man to play wide receiver for them. The 49ers already had dealt Nate Allen and Windlan Hall to Bud Grant for Steve Lawson, the offensive guard. It was popularly described as a ten-strike for the Vikings, but the 49ers weren't kicking. They had adequate strength in their secondary and desperately needed offensive line support. So in October the 49ers' Monte Clark agreed to trade Sammy Johnson, a young, powerful and willing fullback to the Vikings in exchange for Jimmy Lash.

From Jeff Siemon's journal

Thursday, October 21   I read about the trade for Jim Lash today. It was a surprise. I remember Jim since his rookie year, when he had come early before camp and we worked out together. We had another chance to get to know each other in Fred Zamberletti's physical therapy office in St. Paul, when Jim had a knee injury and I was trying to rehabilitate a pulled calf muscle. I not only accompanied him to practice but we worked out together. We respected each other. Although we never spent any time together in a social way, I think we had a closeness. I was saddened to see him go. With Ahmad coming to Minnesota it was inevitable that Jimmy would lose his job. Did I say inevitable? I suppose it is in retrospect, but just six weeks ago I would have thought Jimmy more secure.

Two things happened. Ahmad Rashad revealed himself to be a great player. I thought in that situation that Jim could be a strong backup receiver. But he was still playing without a contract, and with the trading deadline coming up, the handwriting should have been there. But when you like a fellow and get comfortable having him around, you don't see it that clearly. So he was gone at practice today. And here again, although he had been a starter for several years and was a popular guy, it was almost as though he had never

112

been there and as if few people—superficially at least—missed him. Nothing was said. Practice as usual.

A ball player acts this way to insulate himself from the unpleasant. He may be Jimmy some day, or Willie Spencer, the big young fullback who was cut a couple of weeks ago.

The social order and the macho codes may require those public postures. But Siemon understood that the sense of loss among friends and teammates—sometimes the word was brothers—sank deep.

Jim Lash's departure meant a closetful of unused clothes in the apartment he shared with Chuck Foreman. He didn't have time to pack before reporting to San Francisco. Foreman didn't moon about the sudden removal of Jim Lash from the comfortable fraternity they shared. A $100,000-a-year bachelor football player does not fear a monastic life. But he did miss his old roommate.

"Anytime they tell you about the glamor of pro ball," he told a friend, "think of Jimmy. He was with us every day, then all of a sudden he's gone. I talked to him by phone the night he heard the news. He was visiting in Akron. I told him how bad I felt. He said, 'Just another ball club. If it isn't this one it'll be another.' Nobody asked him if he wanted to leave Minnesota and go someplace else. They said, 'Go, Jimmy,' and he went."

In 1976, when there was still no basic player agreement, the all-pros like Foreman negotiated. The Jimmy Lashes went when they were told. For Foreman it was part of the greening of a professional in his fourth season. It might have explained his strident statements on his own salary dispute with the Vikings in Pasadena two months later.

Some time before that, in a reflective mood, he could talk calmly about ambition, insecurity and his own search for a larger identity in a context which most pro football fans decline to recognize. The fan sees them as highly paid prima donnas. "Give them $100,000 and it's not enough. They yell for freedom, but who's got them in chains? I'd love to be shackled to

$100,000. It's the stiff who buys the ticket who pays for their fancy cars. He's the guy who should be bellyaching, not the ball player."

"But ball players are very human guys," Foreman said. "Here's the way the player thinks, and any fan who complains about the ball player's salary would think the same way: You look around at what some of the name athletes are getting in your league and other leagues. You always find yourself comparing, trying to put a value on your accomplishments. I guess you call that market value. I look at mine, then I look up at the TV and I see O. J. running around for a car-rental outfit and other guys doing things with shaving cream and panel trucks, and I say, 'Hey, where's Chuck Foreman?' What I want out of it is enough to be independent when it's over. I want to go into some kind of business that's best for me, that I can run in my good time."

A friend reminded him that very few enterprisers in America, including millionaires, reach that kind of utopia.

"Maybe that's right," he said. "I'm not sure what that business is for me. So I'm looking around, a ball player looking for a clover field, like a lot of other ball players. One difference is that I don't want to be a millionaire or have myself plastered everywhere. I don't think I could ever do all the things Francis Tarkenton has done even if I had the money to start with. And I know if I just corked around for pleasure I couldn't do all the things that Jim Marshall has done. I'm not going to go into the mountains or jump out of airplanes. I'm quieter. I'm not sure I've found Chuck Foreman as a person yet, or maybe the best Chuck Foreman, because that's what I think I'm really looking for. I'm restless about that."

Once he imagined himself a high school teacher counseling the young and troubled, imparting his street sense, tempering it, being a good brother and father to people who needed that. Was this new entrepreneur Chuck Foreman a better person than that?

It isn't a judgmental question. A few years ago he talked seriously of his intentions to quit pro football after three or four years of it. He was going to make enough money to buy a home for his parents and then recede into the life of a counselor and teacher.

He bought the home for his parents and gave them all he had promised himself he would. He returned to Miami to pick up the discarded books and resume his education. But being a star in professional football interceded. What he needed most was no pressure. All summer and fall there were pressures to make it, to be all-pro, to win football games for the Minnesota Vikings, to help get them into the Super Bowl, to win it. That meant the pinnacle for the professional football player. And when the pressures finally relaxed, he wanted to luxuriate in the serenity of no pressure, to drift for a while, to travel, to listen to music, to ride the van coast to coast. It was a good life; was there anything awfully bad about the football player chasing the sun for a few months?

Not at all. But it also meant the slow diluting of his idealism. Not all of his idealism, certainly; he still did things for kids and spent for his parents.

"But time and the way things happen change your goals and outlook," he said. "I'm making good money now. If I stay healthy, I'll do even better. You have to consider what you can reap from your life. There's nothing unclean about making money, is there? Just about everybody I know would like to make a lot of money. It doesn't make the ball player greedy if he wants to do the same thing.

"I look at football differently now. A couple of years ago I wasn't especially proud looking ahead to ten or twelve years of pro ball, no matter how well it paid. Now I'm comfortable with it. I suppose the salary makes you more comfortable. Why be a hypocrite? Football, the way it's set up for me now, is a good life which I can build on. I work hard at it. And you pay a price. Cheapshot guys gun for you. I've got a sore shoulder right now, which isn't going to run me into a hospital and shouldn't keep me out of any games, but it's there. Whether it's sore or not, you better hit somebody."

Like most professional football players, Foreman quickly learned about the mortality of the game: the absence of pure heroism and the recognition that everybody in it bleeds. Not many of them play very well when injured, but most of them play. It is not so much a code; it is the realization of where the money comes from. Yet there are qualities—and Foreman is one of those who sees them—that distinguish the pros who consistently win.

The Vikings' one-time quarterback, Joe Kapp, explained it convincingly enough that a couple of his old teammates clipped it.

"Everyone wants to win," he said, "supposedly. But it's not really true. Some people say they want to win. They'd like to win. But they don't know how to win. To put it better, they're afraid to win. I mean they're afraid to do what you have to do to win. It's more than knowing the requirements of your position. You still need something more, because all the other guys know their jobs, too. To win you got to do the extra things. Hit harder. Work more. Think better. Be hungrier. You don't have to have the most talent. Take what you do best. Perfect it. Stay at it. Plug. Like Grant says, saw wood. Don't stop. You'd be amazed how many times you win because some place, one of their guys stopped."

The judgments the ball players make of each other in the locker room and on the field are seldom couched in absolutes. There are no superbums around them, and not many superpeople either. Because they know their own fallibilities well, they rarely hesitate to reveal a teammate's.

From Jeff Siemon's journal

Saturday, November 6 I did a tape recording for the Channel 9 George McKenzie show and drew the usual questions about the responsibilities of the middle linebacker. I compared it with the quarterback position on offense and said middle linebackers probably had to know more about the overall game plan than the other defensive players. Most of our defensive formations are called from the bench, but the middle linebacker does have to be involved in the strategy and tactics, and he makes some decisions himself.

Well, Wally Hilgenberg and Roy Winston, who locker on either side of me, took my remarks as their text the next day. The conversation was moving along pretty well on another subject when I noticed Roy was putting on a baseball jersey that you can wear during the game if you want. He asked me what I thought he should wear, because he was afraid of getting cold. Roy hasn't been playing of course, and he often jokes about that himself. So I laughed and said, "Yeah, Roy, I think you better wear it." I meant no malice. But maybe it would have been better if Wally had used that line. Roy takes it better from Wally than from me, although we get along extremely well.

Anyhow, Winston looked at me and his eyes got narrow. He didn't look mean, but he did look a little retaliatory. "I heard you on the show, defensive quarterback," he said. I'm such a sensitive guy myself I couldn't help letting something like that tilt me a little. And then Hilgenberg chimed in, "I see you were selling a new product on the show," he said, being very confidential.

"What was that?" I asked.

"Bullshit," Wally said. He smiled brilliantly.

It was one of those little crosses to bear before the game.

Few of the Vikings' star players attracted as much genuine bewilderment as Ron Yary, the great offensive tackle.

There is a theory about offensive linemen. They are the most nearly programmed creatures in pro football, precise in their movements, restricted in their zones of combat. The rules are specific on how they must conduct their biceps, fists and forearms. Because they play in a very structured world, responding to numbers and blocking calls, they are inward thinkers and orderly in their habits. Their hostilities are just as real and

117

probably a lot more intense than the incendiary wraths of the defensive rushers. They are therefore likely to be introspective, brooders with a mean edge to their intellects.

This stereotype, if it is valid, might have been created by Ron Yary.

Long ago he accepted a truth expressed by his offensive line coach, John Michels: "Unless the offensive lineman wipes out the guy in front of him, or gets in the way, or grabs him by whatever is available, the play will break down. But it may also break down because the running back screwed up or the quarterback did, or somebody made a super play on defense. But when they parcel out blame, it's usually the offensive lineman who is in the dock."

For years people knew Yary was in the game only when he was announced the villain of a 15-yard penalty. He seethed about that, too. And whether his disposition turned him into an offensive lineman or vice versa, he seemed to walk to his private drummer in a way that occasionally attracted double takes and lifted eyebrows from his teammates. Most football players, for example, shave when the work day is done. However, one Sunday . . .

From Jeff Siemon's journal

Sunday, November 7 We were sitting around before the game, concentrating as ball players do, getting psyched up. It was all very quiet. Wally went back to the johns and then came back and said, "You'll never guess what I saw."

When Hilgenberg tells you that, you'd better be ready for a small jolt. "It was Yary," he said. "Five minutes before we run out on the field and everybody else is examining his soul, Yary is standing there in front of a mirror *in full uniform* shaving his face!"

Some other defensive player, and I won't identify him, said he was surprised Ron wasn't also brushing his teeth.

The linebacker and his family on the lawn of their suburban home in Minneapolis. Jeff, Dawn, Jeff Jr., 3, and Maile, 2. (*Minnesota Vikings*)

Nate Allen storms from the flank to block Tom Dempsey's field goal attempt on a play that ended with Bobby Bryant racing 90 yards to score the Vikings' first touchdown in the NFC title game against Los Angeles. (*The Minneapolis Star and Tribune Co.*)

Invariably at his best in the big games, Viking all-pro halfback Chuck Foreman lances inside the Redskins' Jake Scott in the Vikings' 35—21 division playoff victory over Washington. (*Minnesota Vikings*)

Congestion corner — Sien (center), Autry Beamon a Wally Hilgenberg roll back Rams on the goal line. Jim B telsen rides blocker John C pelletti to oblivion. The Vikis stopped the Rams on two ser starting with first down an yard from the goal line. T played to a 10—10 tie in September game. (*Minnes Vikings*)

The soaring Matt Blair blocks a Chicago Bear conversion attempt to provide the Vikings' victory margin, 20–19. The Vikings' extraordinary success blocking enemy punts, field goals and extra points helped thrust them into an early dominance of the Central Division race. (*Minnesota Vikings*)

Despite Joe Lavender's golf gloves and his goal line lunge, Viking rookie Sammy White catches a touchdown pass from Fran Tarkenton in their playoff game. (*The Minneapolis Star and Tribune Co.*)

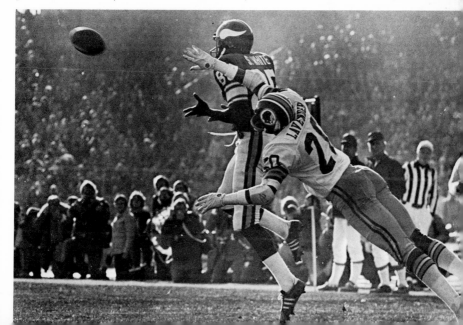

Francis Tarkenton guns over the line to tight end Stu Voigt while bodyguard Chuck Goodrum (68) discourages an enemy tackle. (*Minnesota Vikings*)

SUPER BOWL ACTION: Kenny Stabler sprints out to elude Viking rush, scanning his receivers on the move. His passes in the first half to Dave Casper and in the second half to Fred Biletnikoff broke the game open. *(Minnesota Vikings)*

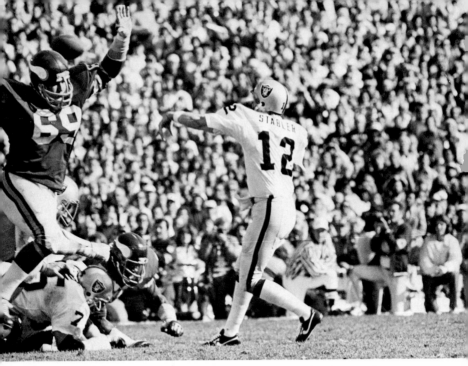

SUPER BOWL ACTION: Kenny Stabler lofts a pass ahead of the onrushing Doug Sutherland. *(Minnesota Vikings)*

SUPER BOWL: Rose Bowl scoreboard declares the dominance of the Oakland Raiders by the second quarter. Oakland led 16−0 with three minutes of the half remaining and had a statistical advantage that could only be described— to the fan in ice-packed Minnesota—as appalling. *(Minnesota Vikings)*

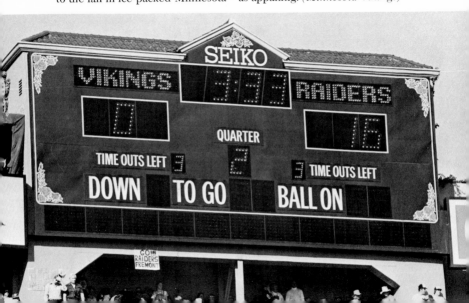

Marshall's career tends to chal-
ge science's insistence that
re is no such thing as an inde-
uctible man. When they
shed the tabulations in 1976
rshall had played in his 236th
secutive NFL game, a record.
ctors, coaches—and offensive
kles who play against him—
e in the general amazement.
has been adventurer, club-
se mimic, and a great football
er. (*Minnesota Vikings*)

icis Tarkenton faced the attri-
s of 16 years in pro football
rterbacking in 1976, missed
ing a game because of injury
he first time, and limped in
through the Super Bowl. But
mained the master of his craft,
ing style somewhat, but not
zest and resourcefulness that
characterized his quarter-
ing since his first year in the
. (*Minnesota Vikings*)

The chiseled good looks of Bobby Bryant are not familiar in the all-star galleries of pro football. He has been injured severely a half dozen times, but by one important measurement of the pro football cornerback—the ability to make the big play—Bryant is excelled by few in the business. He beat the Rams in the NFC title game by running 90 yards with a blocked field goal, and intercepting a probable touchdown pass in the final minutes. (*Minnesota Vikings*)

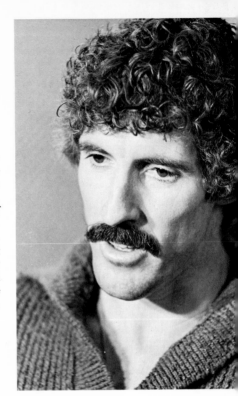

His religious faith, and consiste sound and powerful linebacki earned Jeff Siemon a title—Mini for the Defense. Siemon found it n amusing than impressive, althoug finds football generally a serious b ness, and his play reflects that tude. He fought off injury to pla the NFC title game and delivered of the finest performances of his reer in the Super Bowl. (*Minne Vikings*)

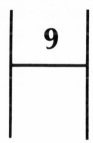

9

Conceded the Central Division title in August, the Vikings observed the formalities by clinching it in November. While the results satisfied their fans, their methods demoralized them.

Their assignment against the Seattle Seahawks at Metropolitan Stadium, for instance, seemed uncomplicated on the surface. The Seahawks were nine weeks old as a professional football team; they stood fourteenth in defense against rushing in the National Football Conference and fourteenth against passing. These figures were of some small significance since there were only thirteen other teams in the National Football Conference. And yet over the past few weeks the Vikings had acquired great ingenuity in turning a sure thing into a bloodchilling adventure.

Something about the simplicities of life touched a rebellious chord in this football team. Maybe it needed a challenge, and the most towering challenge in November was to turn a game with the Seattle Seahawks into an epic. But the Vikings overcame those odds with great resolution. They not only carried the game into the final minute, they nearly blew it in their own ball park to a team that didn't even exist a few months before.

Trailing, 27–21, in the closing minutes, the Seahawks moved to the Viking 1-yard line behind quarterback Jim Zorn. On fourth down Seattle ran a tight-end delay and had John McMakin alone in the end zone for the winning touchdown. But Carl Eller, struggling in a midseason slump, instinctively got in the way and momentarily obscured Zorn's vision. The young quarterback lobbed the ball to the still undiscovered McMakin, who suffered the predictable fate of first-year franchise tight ends: He turned the wrong way and missed the ball. And a minute later, on third and nine from the Viking end zone, Francis Tarkenton bailed out his sleepwalking football team by escaping the vengeance of Bob Lurtsema and throwing upfield to Steve Craig for a first down.

Afterward Lurtsema pretended to be morose over the events of the afternoon, but he lacked credibility. How could the people's benchrider be sad after 48,000 people stood up at halftime and howled their unflinching love? Lurtsema's friends even imported a German police dog to do a reenactment of one of his most popular commercials, one in which Lurtsema impersonating Superman is shagged crossfield by the dog.

The dog might have been influenced by the Viking defense. He made a couple desultory sniffs and then sat down on the sidelines.

From Jeff Siemon's journal

Wednesday, November 17 It really made you wonder where reality is in this whole nutty season. We now stand 8-1-1. We are going to win the Central Division title, so you can say we are two playoff games from the Super Bowl. But everybody on the defense is pretty despondent. And the fans act as though we've wrecked their illusions. It's pretty hard to get yourself oriented.

I remember talking a few days before the game to Jocko Nelson, the linebacker coach. He said he wanted it to be my best game. Both of us knew exactly what he meant. Jack Patera, the Seattle coach, was the Vikings' defensive line coach my first four years here. Jack was and is a good coach. He has a good mind and was well thought of by the defensive linemen. But while he was with the Vikings he was protective of the linemen and tended to be overly critical of the linebackers. All of the linebackers felt some resentment about that. In terms of a coach-player relationship, I never got along very well with Jack Patera for that reason. So there was a little extra flavor to the game as far as I was concerned.

As it turned out, we played just about as well as we had to. The offense once more rescued us. One thing for certain, we underrated Seattle. Whatever else we did, I know I didn't play my best game. It wasn't as bad as the one against Detroit, but sooner or later we're going to have to reestablish some fire and unity on defense. Having said that, I have to look at the record: 8-1-1. Why am I groping for solutions?

Look at Carl Eller. And it's fascinating to see him try to right himself because there aren't any football players I respect more than Carl Eller. In big games he has just been tremendous over the years. I remember talking to him after we lost the playoff game to Dallas last December. He said, "Well, Jeff, that's just about it." And I said, "you mean you're not going to play any more?" He said, "No, that's not it; I will, but it's so tough to get it up week after week now." He thought, in other words, that in the future he couldn't make the ultimate commitment every game. That was honest. I think Bud Grant sees that and has accepted it because Moose really is a great force in this team's continuity.

I've often seen Grant quoted as saying, "Eller will play ordinary games against ordinary players. You've got to be really good before he figures you deserve his full attention."

But then I noticed that it was Carl Eller who had the intuition and the mobility to see that double tight end movement behind the line on the goal line and to get into the pattern and disrupt it for the critical play of the game. He didn't touch a player or the ball, but he saved us. Even on a rather bad day he had something to give the team. Which just might explain why we're 8-1-1 even though the critics can't understand why and some of our opponents can't.

There is some soul-searching going on on this team and people aren't playing as well as they could or should, myself included. You hear speculation among the players about possible changes. The situation is so novel, with our defense playing badly but with the team on the verge of winning a division title, that Bud Grant himself got momentarily confused.

He was talking to us after the game and he wanted to be sure we got the significance of the afternoon—that we knew we played less than we could, but that the scoreboard was how they paid off. And then he said, "Remember, you never have to apologize for losing."

Which just about made the afternoon one long shaggy dog story.

Despite the disarray, the Vikings headed for Milwaukee the third week of November to ratify their pre-season designation as division champions in a game with Green Bay. Siemon told his roommate, Fred Cox, that he was frankly nervous. Cox frowned in surprise. Jeff Siemon on airplanes, buses, the sideline, in the huddle, on the line of scrimmage, was almost always the pillar of tranquility.

"The Packers," Cox said, "can't be that tough to get you jittery." It wasn't the Packers, Siemon explained; it was the prospect of another siege in a strange hotel. A month ago, searching for deodorant, Siemon had gotten locked out of his room in the Philadelphia Hilton and nearly missed the team bus. Their next road game was in Chicago, where they would stay in the Water Tower Hyatt House.

From Jeff Siemon's journal

Saturday, November 20 I thought Philadelphia was bad on Sunday morning, but I almost fainted in Chicago. We had a pre-game meal scheduled at 8:30 A.M., so I got up at 8:10. Cox, who claims all kickers are a little dippy in their habits, confirms this by usually getting up around 6:30 A.M. and going to the coffee shop to talk to whoever is available. He told me years ago that one Sunday the only other person around that early was the kicker from the other team. I'll withhold judgment on that.

Cox was long gone from our room, and I had gotten dressed and was sitting on the edge of my bed tying my shoes. I was wearing a suit made in Hong Kong, not a very expensive suit, one that cost somewhere around $125. As I was doing my shoes, my pants had crept up—and I heard them rip from one end of the crotch to the other.

It wasn't the kind of rip you could get away with. It was a big, oceangoing rip that ran one-half of the way up my rear end. There was just no mistaking the fact that I had a tremendous rip in the seat of my pants, and there was no way I could hide it. I was panic-stricken because I was away from home, it was Sunday morning, and I didn't have a second pair of pants. If I didn't show for the team breakfast on time it would mean one of Bud's fines. I had about twenty minutes to rescue the situation.

My first move was to call housekeeping. I asked them to send someone with a needle and thread. About five minutes later a little lady who spoke Spanish and very little English came up with a needle and thread. She just sort of stood there in the doorway with this needle poised, obviously uncertain of my condition.

I tried to make myself as obscure as possible. At first I told her I would do the sewing. She said something about a machine, and I assumed she meant a sewing machine. I told her I had only fifteen minutes, and she assured me this was enough time. So we went downstairs on the service elevator. All the way down I kept staring high on the elevator door, doing my best to look in command of the arrangements, but I was really sweating. There were a couple of women on the elevator, which didn't make it any easier.

It was suggested I go to the men's room and hand out my pants. This I did. There was a young Mexican guy in there, probably a workman, and he just couldn't figure out this scenario. There I sat on this bench with a vest, a suitcoat, freshly shined shoes, sox, and my underwear.

Time passed, and more time. It was getting to be touch and go on the breakfast deadline. With about three minutes left I looked out the door, and one of the girls relayed to the Spanish lady the message that I was getting nervous about the time. I think that offended her

123

sense of artistry because she screamed something back.

But a minute later the pants arrived. I put them on, carefully, and then tore to the dining room, where breakfast was served thirty seconds later.

In Milwaukee the Sunday morning jinx that hounded Siemon's movements relented. He was troubled by no locked doors or mangled trousers. He did, however, contract a case of diarrhea. The flu that had assaulted a dozen teammates earlier in the week now, four hours before game time, chose to afflict Jeff Siemon.

"Can you imagine how your Sunday mornings would be going," Fred Cox speculated, "if you were an atheist?"

Siemon thanked his roommate for the consoling thought.

By kickoff time, however, Jeff's health had been restored, together with that of the Viking defense in general. The rehabilitation was assisted by the presence of Carlos Brown as Packer quarterback, and by the Packer offense's punchless character. Brown was a manly and dedicated figure in the Packer backfield. But he was, after all, a tight end in college. In relief of the injured Lynn Dickey he carried into this, his first professional starting assignment, a record of three completions in eight passing attempts.

The Vikings thus had no scouting book on Brown. It was a deprivation they managed to survive, 17–10, on the strength of a revived Minnesota defense. The offense passed often—43 times—but inconspicuously. The most decisive blow struck all day by the offense, in fact, was a 30-yard pass which Tarkenton aimed for Ahmad Rashad. It flew five yards over Rashad's forlorn fingertips to wind up in the clutches of Chuck Foreman on the Green Bay 8. With 11 seconds of the half remaining, Tarkenton threw to Robert Miller for the touchdown that was ultimately decisive.

"Imagine my surprise," Rashad said later, "to see the ball being caught by Chuck."

"Imagine my surprise," Tarkenton said, "to see Foreman in the vicinity."

"Nothing Francis does," Foreman said, "surprises me. I thought he was throwing to me all along."

On second thought, Tarkenton discovered a design to what the unaided eye would call blind accident.

"We may have created a Frankenstein's monster here," he theorized. "Some of our receivers know my style so well they get to be mind readers. They all head for where they think I'm going to throw the ball. Sometimes it gets congested down there. When I deliberately threw the ball into the ground in the second period and got a penalty, I half expected Voigt to catch it before it hit the ground."

Of such solidarity are division champions forged.

The game over, the Vikings trudged into the dressing room to enjoy a few minutes of reflection. It passed for the celebration of their eighth division title in nine seasons. The scene constituted one of the memorable non-riots in the history of NFL title clinchings. Moose Eller made a valorous attempt at producing moderate joy by shouting, "Way to go, Vikes!" He spoke in a restrained baritone that almost but not quite carried across the room. A few of his colleagues looked up with forgiving smiles. You make allowances for your friend's quirks.

"It's not that we don't feel real pride winning the division," one of them explained. "But we've done it a lot, and we've done it pretty early. If you celebrate this, you'd also have to celebrate Wednesdays and paying the telephone bill."

From Jeff Siemon's journal

Wednesday, November 24 It was another one of those unglamorous games that seem to bother our fans. But it was very important for the defense to play a sound game, and it did. After the game Francis Tarkenton walked up to Jim Marshall, shook his hand, and said, "Thank you guys for carrying the load." He was saying that things balance out. The two teams, offense and defense, rib each other, and sometimes it cuts pretty deep. But when the doubts become too severe, all you have to do is look at the standings: 9-1-1. I'll take that.

But it wasn't exactly a pulsating afternoon. One of the guys who was especially annoyed was Doug Sutherland, who claimed he was getting legwhipped by Gale Gillingham, the Packers' former all-pro guard. Gillingham has lost much of his old effectiveness, especially after laying out a year, but he still plays a very presentable game. In Doug's view, though, a lot of it was illegal. We were back in the defensive huddle during the TV timeout and Sutherland was yelling his head off at Gillingham, threatening all sorts of destruction. It wasn't idle talk, either. Doug is a pretty ornery sort of guy on the line of scrimmage. He was demanding that Gillingham stop whatever he was doing and he didn't care who heard him.

Somebody in the huddle told Doug to shut up, that all he was doing was getting Gillingham mad and we could do without that. Doug really wasn't impressed by that. "What the hell do you want me to do?" he said. "The guy is legwhipping me." I have no reason to believe he wasn't, but whatever was happening must have stopped because Sutherland was quiet the rest of the game. Quiet and extremely rough and efficient. He's a tough football player, often underrated because of the reputations of some of the more established stars around him.

John Brockington played emotionally again for the Packers, but I'll never be able to explain what's happened to this fellow. He's a real dilemma. Here's a guy who had three great years, over 1,000 yards. Then suddenly he's an ordinary back. I know he had some contract troubles and there were some hard feelings. Later he was benched. He's been healthy now, but he can't get back to where he was. Maybe that should tell me all over again it's an eleven-man game. Maybe the basic difference between John Brockington today and the John Brockington of three years ago is the Packer offensive line. That would make it not so much a dilemma after all.

We got to face Dave Osborn, of course. Old Oz, our teammate for so many years. He came in in the second half in some short-yardage situation. On one of them, as we lined up Wally Hilgenberg began yelling, "You better hold on to the ball, Candoo; we're comin' after you." Cando is Ozzie's home town in North Dakota. Wally wouldn't let up. "Don't cough it up, Candoo." You could see Ozzie trying to fight off the smile on his face. They gave him the ball on one play and he went up high trying to get the first down on what we call a flyover. Jim Marshall and I plugged it up pretty well and Ozzie bounced outside to meet Jeff Wright, his old roommate. Jeff just smothered him. He did everything but tie the rope around Ozzie's legs and feet and come up in record time.

This game does get to be a rough way to make a living. I'm sure Ozzie could tell you that.

So could Doug Sutherland.

Bud Grant's finely tuned antennae informed him that his football team was at that stage of its orderly thrashings where it deserved some act of humanitarianism.

Bud Grant would be the agent of such service. The Vikings' next opponent was San Francisco on a Monday night in San Francisco. It allowed them an extra day of rest, but Bud Grant asked himself: Why not reward this honorable football team with three whole days of rest on Thanksgiving Day week? Their families will be overjoyed. Small hurts will mend. The team will glow with gratitude. The shift will thrust San Francisco and the game of the week in front of the television millions and recapture the team's intensities of weeks ago.

Grant announced his decision after the usual Monday film meeting. It was met with widespread approval. It was agreed all around that the Minnesota Vikings would revive themselves in full view of the multitudes on Monday night.

For three days they lodged in Ricky's Hyatt House, one of those pentagon-style haciendas graced by five nearby shopping centers. It was attractive, but it had a desperate need for floor-plans for disorganized guests lost in the corridors without navigational aids.

The California sun delivered as advertised, comforting the chilled warriors from the northern steppes. They congratulated Grant on his shrewd perception of the jock psychology. Siemon himself adopted the robes of the cordial good host, since this was home terrain. His Stanford team had quartered in this very inn, and the Vikings on Saturday drilled at Stanford.

The occasion called for the grand gesture, so he invited the linebackers to be his guests for dinner at Mings, one of the finest Chinese restaurants in America. Thus replenished, Grant's football team stood ready on November 29 to demonstrate to the masses its rediscovered verve.

But the Viking defense got buried under the cleats of two running backs named Delbert Williams and Wilbur Jackson.

The Viking defense gave up 317 yards on the ground, an embarrassment so bad it needed some form of shared guilt. This was provided by the Viking offense, which was totally disrupted by Cleveland Elam and Jimmy Webb, two defensive linemen who were not exactly international idols. The score was 20–16, but the score was a fraud.

From Jeff Siemon's journal

Tuesday, November 30   A reporter asked me afterward what's the matter with the Vikings against the run. I've heard that for four years, and it's answered in a half dozen ways that usually satisfy nobody. Every team in football is vulnerable to the run in some games. With us, I think, the problem is physical. Unless we're fired up we give a lot away physically to some of the teams. We don't have the biggest guys; in fact our defense may be the lightest in pro football. Unless we're motivated and the other team has a good running game going, the worst may happen. But I didn't imagine we could give up 317 yards.

Bud addressed the squad the next day. Same old Bud, no panic in his voice. We're still in the playoffs. He said we had been humiliated, though, and he seemed to be waiting for somebody on the team to come forward and say, "Hey, when does somebody around here start to get worried or excited?"

The somebody turned out to be a man you might not have nominated. He gave his name as Chuck Foreman.

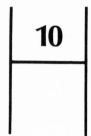

10

Chuck Foreman asked for permission to address the squad.

It was not an ordinary request, but it was one the coach willingly granted. He had gathered his team for the usual Friday afternoon announcements at the close of practice week for the next-to-last game of the regular season. Foreman raised his hand just before the herd broke for the dressing room.

His speech is not likely to become a memorization exercise in Eighth Grade English. Those who heard it agree it was easily surpassed in eloquence by the American commander's reply to the Germans at Bastogne. For brevity it came in slightly under Santa Claus' instructions to his reindeer.

Foreman never claimed to be a spellbinder. But he had decided earlier in the week that there was a leadership gap on the football team, for all the elder superstars around him. He, Chuck Foreman, affable fullback and former locker room churchmouse, would now be a head-pounding, butt-kicking leader.

Many of his teammates were impressed and a few were amused. All of them had great admiration for Chuck Foreman's work between the sidelines and his habit of delivering some of

130

his best football in playoff games. It was a trait that improved everybody's bank deposits. Foreman, therefore, was a man who deserved their attention.

He had talked about the situation privately earlier in the week. He said he was disgusted by the debacle in San Francisco and afraid what it might foreshadow for December.

"We were unbelievably bad. They hit and blocked and tackled like it mattered to them, and they're out of the playoffs. We're in the playoffs, and we played like it didn't matter worth a damn. We went out there like we were expecting them to fall down watching us. What we've got to find out all over again is that when you play pro football, and you want to win a championship, you just got to go out there and kick rear ends. You got to do it every play. We figure we're a bunch of cool cats who can win on finesse. How many teams win the playoffs on finesse? We nearly got beat this year by teams we should have beaten by 50 points.

"Don't tell me a lot of teams have got talent as good or better than the Minnesota Vikings. I don't believe it. We got as much or more than anybody in football. We better change our attitude on this team fast. I don't care if the guys on this team are tired of hearing it, they better wake up and start getting emotional. I'm saying it again, and the next time may be too late."

In another part of the room stood Moose Eller, who like the republic itself and the Rock of Ages had survived several calamities of the kind now being predicted by Chuck Foreman. Although a friend and brother, he responded to different vibrations. "I can't attach too much importance," Carl Eller said, "to losing to San Francisco in a game that means nothing. This was their Super Bowl. Our's is ahead."

Possibly in expectation of that reaction, Foreman stood in the players' circle the Friday before the second Green Bay game and screamed, "let's go crazy on these m----------s!"

The Packers had done nothing especially wicked to earn this uncomplimentary designation. Foreman didn't say they had. He was trying to build a frenzy.

131

On this football team? Foreman had to be reading the wrong horoscopes. These were comfortable, successful businessmen ball players. Wasn't that the profile? For the Vikings an emotional experience was depositing their playoff checks. Somebody said that one of the few things that turned them on was watching the icicles lengthen on the goalposts. And this team was now going to go crazy against those m-----f----n' Green Bay Packers?

Not only the Green Bay Packers, Foreman and his partners--in-incitement insisted, but the Miami Dolphins the following week and the three playoff teams after that, up to and including the one in Pasadena.

Foreman's chief accomplices were Ahmad Rashad, Nate Allen and—an improbable fourth to complete the quadrangle —Jerry Burns, the waspish offensive coordinator. Somewhere in the middle of the season Rashad had extracted a crusader's chant out of some forgotten locker room of his travels. Rashad was a suave, self-possessed sort of guy, a man who could look supremely graceful wrestling a greased hippo. He was also jivey and exuded charismatic qualities that inspired Foreman.

Nate Allen was less charismatic but more jivey. From the beginning Nate pined for the one property missing in his wholesome new surroundings, and that was some functional hell raising and soul celebrating. Stubby Eason's stereo, which had been quickly commandeered by the groovier members of the team, provided the wall-shaking decibels needed to transport the Vikings into the hear-and-now musically. Gradually Foreman, Rashad, Allen and others introduced the boogaloo and go-crazy chant into the Viking pre-game rites. The campaign did not enrapture all hands and eardrums immediately, but it established beachheads. Slowly it expanded on the consciousness of the starched-collar traditionalists. It was like bringing a disco party into the convention of the Daughters of the American Revolution. Slowly the walls creaked and tumbled. What the hell; it was a change.

"We gotta be one, man!" Foreman would yell. "We gotta play

like crazy. Everybody play like crazy. Francis, you gonna play like crazy? Tora, Tora, Tora."

The tycoon quarterback from the old Confederacy could see no reason why he shouldn't play like crazy—which, after all, used to be called scrambling.

Burns got caught up in movement. When you went crazy, he informed his offense, it pinned down a lot of people. "If it takes two people to hold down a normal man," he said, "it takes ten people to hold down a crazy man. And when you got eleven guys going crazy, they just don't have enough people on the roster to handle all of those wildmen."

Go crazy, Burns! they yelled.

The Grants and Landrys of pro football had always shunned showy excitement in the grooming of a football team for Sunday. But neither was opposed to emotionalism as such in football. How could they be? When you line up across the line from a 250-pounder you'd better be well-juiced with emotion because it is an unnatural act to throw yourself into that creature. Emotion might lead you onward where logic would tell you to get out of there with all deliberate speed. It was the tinny, artificial bravado that worried people like Grant and Landry.

Was go-crazy artificial?

Grant has not coached for twenty years in pro football by stomping on the enthusiasm of his ball players, especially when it is accompanied by three touchdowns on offense and a couple of goal-line stands the next Sunday.

Bobby Bryant, a guitar-picking tenor, mod in style but reserved in a crowd, evaluated the new gusto.

"It's real," he said. "It's cool. We used to have a rigid attitude and called that professionalism. I don't know if that kind of detached attitude won any football games or lost any. We won a lot. And we had that attitude, so we kept it. Maybe we didn't have enough fun. Who knows? All this stuff is theory anyhow. We could win three or four games with this new spirit and then have everything blow in a big playoff game or even the Super Bowl. Which wouldn't mean the attitude was wrong but just that we lost the ball game. But we have a lot of guys around here looking for a release, some way to let themselves express what they feel about the excitement of playing football. So we really kind of transformed ourselves. I like it. I'm as expressive as a lot of guys. But I like what it's done for this football team. If guys want to run and yip and hug coming off the field, and that gives them release and says what they want to say, I want it. Everything is okay, I guess, short of spiking the football."

After the Nate Allen and Sammy White episodes, nobody was going to go *that* crazy.

From Jeff Siemon's journal

Tuesday, December 7 While everybody was getting ready to go crazy against the Packers, things were surprisingly normal in our corner of the dressing room. They were riding Jim Marshall for missing practice.

Grant makes big allowances for Marshall because of his age and his medical history. That and the fact that Jim seems to be ready most Sundays even if he lays off two or three days a week, which he has been doing a fair part of the season. It came up again before the Packer game, and Jim really got incensed at Alan Page and Carl Eller. He asked Alan how could he say anything about Marshall after he was excused from most of the training camp to study law. And then he got on Moose, who has been notorious for missing days. But this year Jim has seized a commanding lead in the number of practice days missed, though the competition has been tough.

I've been getting plenty of whirlpool time myself. I took a terrific shot in the knee from our old teammate Andy Maurer in San Francisco.

One thing you could have predicted against the Packers: Chuck Foreman wouldn't start. Chuck made that speech after practice about going crazy but he wasn't in the starting lineup two days later. If you miss most of practice you're not going to start, barring some highly unusual circumstances, or if you happen to be Jim Marshall. Grant maintains the policy for two reasons: You really aren't technically ready if you haven't worked most of the week. And it's a message—don't nurse the marginal injuries, or what Bud Grant considers marginal injuries, if you expect to be there when the whistle blows. That applies to no less a star than Chuck Foreman, and it also includes Jeff Siemon. There is not much appeal from the diagnosis of Dr. Bud Grant.

The Vikings didn't go crazy against Green Bay, but they did go 416 yards in total offense, which may have been more rewarding.

They also throttled the Green Bay attack, limiting it to 59 yards in the air and only 140 yards in total. It produced a 20–9 victory which seemed a credit to the newborn evangelism of Foreman and Rashad and the restorative qualities of December. The Vikings always react well to December. Other NFL organizations frankly resent the Vikings in December; they ascribe unfair advantages to them in winter and insist that the Vikings owe much of their ten years of success to windchill factors and fear of frostbite among their opponents.

The theory makes sense until Grant produces some simple mathematics. Most of the Viking divisional titles have been clinched before the Vikings, or their opponents, for that matter, reached December.

While the team has lost some important games at home in December (specifically the playoff games with Dallas, San Francisco and again Dallas), the record supports the meteorologists. Of the eight games they won in their four Super Bowl seasons, seven were played in Metropolitan Stadium in December or even January.

One was played in Dallas. They won there, too, in what may have been the Vikings' finest all-around performance in their sixteen-year history. Still, if Grant is correct in embracing the doctrine about a time and a place for everything, the time and place for the Vikings is December in Minnesota. Most football teams consider it an imposition to be playing football north of Twentynine Palms in winter. Grant recognizes this and exploits it with his well-publicized ban on artificial heat on the sidelines. The coach is so Spartan about it that one of his players said he was surprised Grant allows the Vikings to wear helmets.

A sizeable percentage of Grant's players loathe cold weather and fear it. A few of his stars like Tarkenton openly bootleg heating aids into their crotches, where it is not easy to openly bootleg. Roy Winston spent the better part of fifteen Decembers in Minnesota helplessly cursing the cold and the NFL owners for locating a franchise in Minnesota instead of Death Valley, which is more compatible with Winston's blood viscosity.

None of this disturbs Grant because he is convinced his Eskimo Story over the years has rescued the weakest and emboldened the neediest. His operating thesis about cold weather is that the team most successful in it is the one that ignores it.

At −40 windchill, he admits, this is a challenge. But once a year Grant summons his squad and tells about the Eskimo. If he forgets, his veterans remind him. It is intended for rookies and other aliens in Minnesota who are unfamiliar with the rigors of −40 windchill. Rookie-watching during Grant's annual recital has become one of the spinoff benefits of seniority on the Minnesota Vikings. It has reached a point where some of the vets like Jim Marshall lobby noisily for the Eskimo, looking on the story as a kind of psychological fix.

From Jeff Siemon's journal

Thursday, December 16   Today there was no ugly northwest wind at practice. It wasn't spitting snow, and none of the newcomers to the squad was wondering how the Good Lord expected them to play football in this kind of weather. But at our meeting Bud talked about cold weather football. It's coming to be a performance. Maybe there's some show biz in Bud after all. He said there was no magic about playing in the cold, just a matter of knowing you are going to be cold and accepting it. By popular request, he said, he had been asked to tell about the Eskimos. Applause greeted this remark. Bud Grant the Minstrel spoke.

136

He told about radar stations that were being built high in the frozen country of Canada as warning devices against the Russians. The construction people couldn't keep the American workers on the bulldozers for any length of time no matter how much clothing they put on. Somebody got the idea of trying out Eskimos and teaching them how to run the dozers. Everybody was amazed how the Eskimos could sit on the machines hour after hour without apparent ill effects. The researchers were called in. They made complete physiological studies of the Eskimos in an attempt to find out what there was in the constitution of these people that permitted them to withstand cold where the Americans couldn't.

They did studies of blood types, fatness of the skin, all those areas of physical makeup. They came up with a one-page report. The gist of the report was that the Eskimo was no different from the American. They said he was able to sit on the bulldozer and work all that time without relief because he knew he was going to be cold. He was going to be cold, he accepted it and he functioned in it. The American resented the cold and refused to function in it.

At the Met, Bud said, it's going to be cold in December. We may as well know it. Don't expect relief on the sidelines because we're here to play, not to get warm. So think about football and worry about getting warm later.

A lot of people smiled, but Sammy White, who is a rookie from Louisiana, didn't. It looked like he was shivering already. I think Sammy is one of those guys who will always hate cold weather, will never accept it but will somehow find a way to play well in it.

I must admit that Sammy didn't have his best game of the season against Green Bay at the Met on December 5.

Come to think of it, maybe Grant should have told the story sooner.

The reason he may not have told the story sooner had something to do with the schedule. The Vikings finished the regular season in Miami, where the windchill seldom reaches –40, although it came remarkably close six weeks later.

It was a game where Grant's athletes wanted to nourish a

137

rising momentum they had detected in the game against Green Bay: more going crazy for Foreman, more sawing wood for Grant. They belonged to different generations and used different language, but the idea was about the same. The game once again matched Grant against Don Shula, two of the NFL's coaching masters, and—surprisingly—there was an edge of vengefulness in Grant's intentions despite the mutual respect between them.

Some time before Grant had telephoned Shula on business. Although he is not your typical conversational butterfly, Grant does try to observe the amenities. On this particular day Shula must have been rushed, and he snuffed out the conversation after two minutes. This might have explained why Grant allowed himself to be quoted in a Miami newspaper that week saying he wanted his football team to pile it on Miami. The remark was so uncharacteristic it looked like a typographical error. It may not have motivated the team, but a defensive stand that repelled Miami four times on the 1-yard line did.

Tarkenton's offense responded by matching the world football record for length in one scoring drive. The Vikings went 99 yards and two feet. The odd thing about it was the total lack of suspense once Tarkenton got the first down. It may not have been the only 99-yard, two-foot scoring drive in history, but it certainly was the most predictable. Everything Tarkenton attempted worked for eight yards, sometimes nine and a few times eleven. The game ended when Tarkenton passed into the end zone. They would have spared Bob Griese the embarrassment of a prolonged booing from his devoted public if they had canceled the rest of it. The Vikings won, 29–7.

They suddenly remembered the Eskimo because their next game was at the Met on December 18, against the Washington Redskins in the NFL playoffs. The face they saw in closeup on television Sunday night belonged to the coach of the Washington Redskins. It was filled with anguish and dilemma, doubt and connivance. It was, in other words, the face of a man content in his work and eagerly facing his weekly Armageddon.

"Even if we win big," said Francis Tarkenton, "it's always an ordeal just facing George Allen, let alone beating him."

11

From Jeff Siemon's journal

Tuesday, December 14   After we viewed films of the Miami game some of the veterans gathered at Stubby Eason's home for his annual holiday dinner. His wife Dodie prepared an Italian meal that was just fabulous. We ate around the television set during the second half of the Dallas-Washington game, which decided our opponent for the first playoff game at the Met. Dallas had already clinched a playoff berth and was going to play the Rams. I wanted Washington to win because it was better for the Minnesota Vikings. Most of us thought it would be Dallas, though, especially Wally, who suffered terribly giving 3-to-1 odds. Washington won it with a great fourth quarter. I think we can beat this team decisively.

Dawn and I bought a Christmas tree at Colonial Church Monday night after the party. We decorated it shortly after bringing it home. The children helped, which may be a generous thing to say. Little Jeff took practically all of the beautiful wooden ornaments that Dawn's mother had given us and hung all of them on the bottom branches. After he finished his work and was out of the room, we redistributed them to give the tree some artistic balance that Jeff overlooked.

It was my first day away from football in two weeks, and the thought struck Mommy and me at about the same time: It had been much too long since we spent some time together without the kids. The tree, with lights on it, was in the basement, just a lovely scene. I started a fire in the fireplace, we spread a sheet on the floor beside it and we enjoyed each other for a few hours that night before falling asleep.

The most unkind side to the contempt piled on the football team that lost its fourth Super Bowl in January 1977 was the selective blindness of the critics and the devastated homefolks.

It worked this way:

Fact. Football team loses four times in the game of games. Conclusion: Football team can't win the big game. It must either be choking, it must be getting outcoached or it must have the wrong guy playing quarterback. It deserves our laughs (or our tears).

Fact again. To qualify for the game of games, football team has to win at least two big games which on the day they were played were the most important either team had played all season.

Conclusion: Don't come at me with all these limp and pointless facts.

Who's going to listen?

Maybe the Washington Redskins.

On December 18 the Washington Redskins played the Minnesota Vikings in the game that would qualify one team for the National Football Conference finals. They brought to the game an engrossing group of overage brawlers, wise and brave antiques, some quality players in their prime and a quarterback freshly busted for alleged drunk driving. They also brought a coach renowned for deviousness and his manic preparation for Big Games—or any games. He was a coach who, in his midnight-candle fatigue or despair in midweek, would oblige any inquiring journalist and croak out the litany of disaster his team had overcome. He seemed in fact to draw sustenance from it and would drone and drone. He always gave the impression that a Washington victory would represent an astonishing triumph for abandoned and misused souls over the forces of privilege and comfort.

Having convinced no one, he would deliver his friendless ancients to the soil of their executioners. There they would play like hell and very often win.

Allen's teams are almost always ready for a big football game. Like an impressive number of their NFL rivals, Allen's teams have never won the Big One. In this they are joined by the Los Angeles Rams, Cleveland Browns, Detroit Lions, Cincinnati Bengals, St. Louis Cardinals, San Francisco 49ers, New England Patriots, Buffalo Bills, Chicago Bears, New York Giants, Philadelphia Eagles, Denver Broncos, Houston Oilers and, among others, the Minnesota Vikings. By actual count twenty teams in the NFL have not won the Big One. Most of these have not won middle-sized ones, either; this partially explains their unblemished record in the Super Bowl.

One of them, the Los Angeles Rams, has consistently lost every football game that would have given it access to the Big One. Its chroniclers have analyzed these failures closely and concluded that the Rams lose playoffs because of (a) Bad Luck, closely followed by (b) Minnesota Weather, and (c) Officials' Atrocities.

Excluding the Vikings, of all the teams that have not won the Big One, the Washington Redskins invariably are the most meticulously prepared and the one in the most positive emotional state to play a football game that matters.

Yet on December 18 the Washington Redskins played a team of comparable age, with similar strengths and weaknesses and with a quarterback as widely criticized as their own quarterback. They played on a day so mild it might have been accepted by the Skinny Dippers Association.

And the Redskins got mauled, 35–20. Until they scored two fourth quarter touchdowns, it was the mismatch of the season.

Few football fans have an opportunity to witness a pro game from ground level.

It is something to remember. Every football watcher should be granted one such privilege, if only as a reward for all of the indignities one must bear, from beer suds on the head to half-time shows.

A man from the press box (me) decided the Washington-Viking game would be a game to experience in its natural habitat—and he regretted the fan could not join him.

The fan should be allowed to crouch beside the first down chain crew, watch the quarterback's fingers twitch beneath the center's rump and listen to the cornerback talk to the flanker.

"I'm gonna bust your nuts, man."

The fan should be able to watch the flanker react to this unlovely prospect. There is no reaction. The flanker stares straight ahead, toeing the turf for traction.

The ball slaps into Tarkenton's hands and the dreadnoughts mesh on the line of scrimmage. When it is viewed from the grandstand, there is a rough geometry in their thrashing movement. A pocket forms, wavering, constricting; the quarterback maneuvers inside it. He seems in control, aware of the pressure around him but shrewdly absorbing the currents downfield, the sprinting receivers and the defensive backs.

But when you watch him from 40 feet away, on the ground, the quarterback does not appear shrewd at all. Not even Tarkenton. He is a hunted man who looks wild and abandoned. Bodies fall around him, arms reach for him. A tackle yells at him. He wants to throw—*now*—but one of the bodies has him screened. He ducks his head and a 260-pound end hurtles past him. He lifts his head and, in the same motion, throws.

At precisely this moment he is buried beneath two late-arriving bodies, one of them in an alien uniform, one of them friendly.

The ball whistles 35 yards to the sideline, where it just escapes the fingernails of the flanker, Rashad, who has traded elbow

143

punches with the cornerback, Pat Fischer. They pile into a defenseless photographer and land tangled. Mucous dribbles from Rashad's handsome nose. He blurts a barnyard expletive and walks back to his huddle.

The roar in the stands subsides; it was just another incomplete pass in a football game.

But you couldn't watch it from the sidelines and ever again rip the quarterback for failing to see a receiver wide open on the other side of the field. Or look on the flanker as a man remote, aloof from the combat in the barbed wire.

It's impossible to put 50,000 people on the sideline of a football field, of course, and that is a pity, for there is one dimension of the game that does not disclose itself to the camera or to the grandstand dweller. That is the intimate although oddly impersonal savagery of the game.

The overhead camera cannot probe the eyes of a defensive back to see the desperation when he is being beaten on a pass play. It does not reveal the confusion in an official's eyes when he has lost the play but still must make a decision—and make it emphatically.

Let's say the sideline watcher has played high school football and knows about the physical shocks, the grappling and struggling and the chance of pain. If he has any sophistication as a watcher, he also knows there is nothing especially heroic about many people who play pro football. They are the best because they are bigger, faster or more gifted athletically. They are capable of extraordinary deeds for precisely these reasons. But they are also capable of amateurish breakdowns and failures at critical moments because none of them is impervious to pressure. All of them, sooner or later—and sometimes often—wear the hunted look of the quarterback under duress.

There is not much showtime chic here. The pummeling and grunting and grabbing assert a verdict from the jungle.

From above, a Chuck Foreman may look stylish and breathtakingly fluid. But come down to the 3-yard line of the Washington Redskins, with the Vikings already leading.

On the opening play of the game they have complied with Chuck Foreman's exhortation and gone crazy. They rousted the right side of the Washington line. Brent McClanahan ran 41 yards on the first play, and a minute later Tarkenton passed to Voigt for a touchdown.

They are now on the Washington 3. Foreman takes Tarkenton's handoff and bolts to his left. Kenny Houston, the Washington safety, comes up hard, his head low. Foreman lowers his helmet. You can hear the report and you marvel at how either avoided a broken neck. Houston sprawls. Foreman lunges as he is falling. Two Redskins wrestle with him on the goal line. The official raises his arms. Foreman bounds back as gleeful as a kid with his first gold star. There is nothing childish about the language the Redskins use on the official. "He ain't in yet, you chickenshit. He ain't in *yet.*"

The official runs crisply to plant the ball on the conversion line. He's heard it all before, and he is instructed to tolerate the casual crudities. The Redskins, after all, may have been right. If they threw out a ball player for insulting an official, the field would be empty by the end of the first quarter. Van Brocklin used to call one Italian official "spaghetti-eater" and another "Cyclops" because of his large glasses. He also had more vivid descriptions. And so does Bud Grant. But if they could brush off Dutch, they certainly can handle people like Kenny Houston, Joe Lavender, Pat Fischer and Ron McDole.

McDole is a wine barrel of a man who plays defensive end for Washington. He has great forearms, shoulders and chest and an indelicate girth. His contours and disposition inspire a nickname: Dancing Bear. McDole is one of the esteemed old brawlers of the football frontier called the line of scrimmage, a man with the lumberjack's wariness of the niceties of life. Once in a while you will see him nod or converse when the Vikings' Mick Tingelhoff is in the vicinity. McDole was asked earlier in the week: Was he such a tough guy that he would knock down the godfather of his first-born daughter?

"Yeah, I would," he said. "Tingelhoff. He's the godfather.

Great guy. We used to babysit together while our wives were playing cards. We liked it. It gave us a chance to make the damndest drink you ever saw, with chocolate, bananas, malt and vodka. I liked him so much I named my first son after him. Would I try to knock him on his can? Yeah, I would. I got a credibility problem. If I can hit Tingelhoff hard I got my kids to answer to. If I don't I got George Allen to answer to."

If you weren't standing on the sidelines, you would miss some of the touching little dialogues between McDole and Tingelhoff. You might also miss Joe Lavender's sunglasses, for the young man is actually wearing shades beneath his face bars. He was wearing them on the opening play of the game when McClanahan ran right through Joe's sunglasses and face bars for 41 yards.

Nor would you hear Alan Page's impersonal lecture to the Washington guard who was holding him, or appreciate his retaliation on the next play when he burst into the backfield the moment the ball was snapped, past the flailing arm and chagrined jawbone of the Redskin guard. If you played with Page, or understood him, the play would not surprise you. His teammates contend that nobody plays with more zealotry each game, despite his midweek laments of boredom.

From Jeff Siemon's journal

Friday, December 17   We went to our defensive meeting room to talk about the Redskin offense and Neill Armstrong started going through some defensive theory and philosophy. He was talking about a specific defense and there was a specific line charge that the defensive tackles had to execute. As he was talking he checked with Alan Page: "Okay, Alan?"

There was no response. He said, "Okay, Alan?" again. And then he said, somewhat resigned, "Would somebody wake him up?"

Sure enough, there was Alan sitting in one of the locker stalls as they always do in the meeting rooms, and he was dead asleep. That was a definite first. I've seen players asleep many times, almost every

146

day during films, but I've never seen one asleep at the beginning of a defensive meeting when the coach was going through a defensive play. And in playoff week, of all weeks.

Alan was aroused, of course, and Winston was one of the first to fling a dart. "That's okay, Alan," he said. "It's not a very big game." Alan kind of smiled and shrugged. I don't think he was too worried about getting fined.

To hear Ron Yary and Ed White, you would have to be standing with the chain gangs, but it would be worth it. Many football players splutter and snarl coming off the line. It is the punctuation at the end of the ball player's simple, declarative statement: He is going to hit someone, and he is going to be hit. It is also a nervous release.

Yary is positively creative, especially when pulling out of the line as a downfield blocker. He comes steaming and rasping around the corner, and if sounds could scare, the linebacker would capitulate instantly. White's grunts have a less expressive quality, being acoustically closer to the feeding trough than to the jungle.

There are few Prince Vals in all that turmoil. The objective is survival and victory. Toward these ends, tricks and marginal crimes are allowable. People hold and grab on every play. Defensive linemen pile into the quarterback on the ruse of having too much momentum to stop. A Diron Talbert of the Redskins goes "hut" ahead of Tarkenton's "hut." A stab at confusion, it flops.

If the violence is real and the measures the ball players take are often sly, illegal or wicked, why don't more people get hurt in this continuing mayhem?

Ed White lectures on the subject with great authority. "I think the common denominator is what the trainers would call the adrenalin flow. You're just all puffed up for a ball game. Your level of intensity is so high you're really not conscious of some of the blows. The body is an amazing instrument. It protects against pain when the need is the greatest. When you have to

147

deliver performance, the marginal injury just doesn't register on you. I came into the locker room after a game and whooped it up with the others for a couple of minutes and then sat down to undress. I looked down at my sock, and it was just shredded. There was a big welt there where somebody's cleat had ripped into me. I wasn't even aware of it during the game. After the game it hurt something fierce."

You have to see the game from the ground to recognize some of the subtleties. Paul Krause kneels and catches the ball for Freddie Cox's extra point. As he lowers the ball to the ground on its point, he spins it so the laces will be facing away from Freddie. Nobody ever talks about the holder unless he screws up. But try that little maneuver with a football—and be sure you don't let the ball slip because that means you've blown the conversion and possibly the ball game. Now imagine the ball soggy or slick with cold, and imagine as you are spinning it that there's a 9.6 sprinter bearing down on you from the corner and a 260-pounder blowing up the middle. You know that because nobody is blocking the sprinter, and they can hear the big man in the fifth row of the east bleachers.

From the sideline, Fred Cox's shoe looks perfectly normal because, lucklessly for admirers of intrigue, it is.

From Jeff Siemon's journal

Friday, December 17 All the visiting writers and broadcasters dropped in to see our last big practice before the Redskin game, and it was a show. They were looking for solemn faces and smooth, clipped professional conduct, and they got a variety hour. We had people clowning and doing pantomimes, carrying on with a tremendous looseness and confidence. But nobody messed up the plays when it came time to run our offense and defense, for sure. We also carried out the Fred Cox charade.

In the middle of the week Bud went into one of his red-herring acts. The coaches have noticed for a long time how Mark Moseley, the Washington kicker, seems to drag his foot coming downfield after kicking. They're convinced he has some weight in there to give him extra distance on his kicks, and I'm sure they're right. In training camp Freddie experimented with a metal shank of his own, and it did seem to give him more distance—something Fred admits he needs at this stage of his career. He's never used it in a game.

The league is embarrassed about the business of a doctored shoe because several years ago Tex Schramm of Dallas tried to get shoes standardized. It was a move aimed partly at Tom Dempsey, the clubfooted kicker many pro people believe gets extra distance because of the type of shoe he must wear. Obviously the league isn't going to let itself legislate against a handicapped ball player. So there isn't any enforced rule about the kicking shoe. The only provision is that it should be "manufactured." Once you've got the shoe, evidently you can put anything inside as long as it doesn't show. The league doesn't want that, and it's technically illegal, but the league can't find the language for a rule without disqualifying Dempsey.

So Bud announced at a press conference, making it sound offhand, of course, that Fred just might use his metal shank in the game.

George Allen screamed that Moseley's shoe was as honest as Abe Lincoln's nose and under no circumstances would he let Cox use a doctored shoe. As a matter of fact, he said, he would bring a scale to the game to weigh Fred's shoe.

On the last big day of practice Fred pretended to use it. And he boomed kickoffs like I haven't seen him do for years. Five yards into the end zone, kicking from the 35! Everybody was awed by what they thought was this potential new weapon, including the ball players.

We knew the officials would ignore Allen's demand for a scale, but it was all academic because Cox had no plan to use the shoe in the game. He told me kicking might have felt strange that way and could have induced all sorts of reactions from the ball. Besides, I don't think Fred knew any more than the rest of us what Bud was trying to accomplish (which I assumed had something to do with baiting the NFL front office). Bud has been conducting a personal campaign against Rozelle's office for years. He thinks the officiating is the only unprofessional part of pro football. He also thinks there is overman-

149

agement of the league by the league office and he is constantly building fires under the public relations guys for the Hollywood aspects of pro ball.

So that was behind the Cox shanked shoe ploy—rubbing it into the league for not doing something about Moseley. Grant set the whole thing up in midweek, and most of the writers thought he was stone serious. Three years ago he did the same thing by complaining about sparrows in the high school locker room they gave us for the Super Bowl. For a guy who's so expressionless on the sidelines, Bud does have a creative mind for aggravation.

From the grandstand or in the living room the game seems neatly segmented, the action precisely defined. The players move as diagrammed. It is like a chess game, tidy at a distance despite the hostilities. And yet because it is seen as a performance, it conceals its more private sensations from the camera and the binoculars.

It has very little privacy when experienced up close. Francis Tarkenton gets up after being hit throwing a pass. He waits until attention is focused elsewhere and then tries his leg. He does it carefully. He limps a few strides and then walks off the field, methodically and without a limp.

From the sidelines you could read his mind.

"Nobody has to know I'm hurt."

There was more football to be played, so he played through the third period without a limp. There was time enough for everybody to know about his knee after the ball game.

Jeff Siemon could make no such concealment. He was clearly disabled before the end of the first half.

From Jeff Siemon's journal

Sunday, December 19   Sometimes your body warns of an injury. My leg started getting sore in the first quarter, and it worsened a little each series. On a play where Bobby Bryant intercepted a pass near our goal line, I went to the sidelines and told Fred Zamberletti my leg was getting sore and I thought I might be in danger of a pull.

He gave me a potassium pill and some mixture which I was about to drink when they called us back on the field hurriedly. We were turning down a penalty because the interception put us on our 1-yard-line; instead we were going to give them third down and long yardage, which was a smart decision by Grant. I remember the pill still being in my mouth when I dropped back in pass coverage. I took a step and pop—I felt very intense pain.

I honestly thought someone had thrown something from the stands, like a ball bearing, something small and hard, and it had hit me in the calf. Dr. Lannin once told a story about a guy in the army who had had a similar experience. They were marching someplace and all of a sudden the guy turned around and smacked the man behind him in the jaw, thinking the man had kicked him in the back of the leg. That's the kind of sensation I got. I had to hop to the side because I couldn't put any pressure at all on my leg. I was terribly demoralized. We were playing a great game, and I thought I was having a good one, helping the team. But it wasn't over, and this was the end of the road for me today—and maybe for the season. I tried to submerge this personal disappointment, and asked the Lord to strengthen me in the midst of it. I thought about Amos Martin, who went in to replace me.

Amos is a member of our small prayer group, and one of my closest buddies. I knew how tough football has been on him at times. He hasn't been playing much, but he's a pretty sound football player, very competent. It was so important for Amos that he should play well now, so important for him and the team. And he did well. I couldn't have been more happy for this good friend. He was uncertain here and there, but he would have been inhuman not to be. So the defense played about as well as it had been playing until it gave up two unimportant touchdowns in the fourth quarter.

I wasn't surprised. The locker room before the game had radiated emotion. Jim Marshall was sitting down, throwing a ball back and forth to somebody, and I got in on it. Marshall was throwing the ball so hard he was almost knocking down the receiver. Something about the occasion brought more people into the game. We were throwing the ball back and forth, hard and with purpose, and it was a declaration of something. And when Bud called us to go out on the field, there was the kind of reaction I'd never experienced as a pro player.

It just engulfed you. You said to yourself, "This has to be real. This is no rah-rah. This is a team that has gathered itself for something big, and I just don't know human nature if something big isn't going to happen in the next three hours."

It did, of course. For three quarters it may have been the best football game the Vikings had played for five years. McClanahan's run established the tone. After that you got terrific catches, great blocking, Tarkenton's direction and some really supercharged defensive play that just stampeded Bill Kilmer and buried the Redskins' ground game. We had interceptions by Bobby and Nate Wright. Stu Voigt hauled three guys into the end zone for our first touchdown. It was a surpassing day.

When Nate got back to the bench after his interception, the whole sideline went ecstatic. He's a popular guy and it was a big play.

I joined my teammates in the locker room at halftime, but I had to be wheeled there in a cart. After being taped I dressed and watched the rest from the sidelines in street clothes, which gave me an odd sensation.

Near the end of the game Kilmer threw a little check-off pass to Calvin Hill. Matt Blair came up and made a tremendous hit on him. You could hear it all over the stadium. When he got up Matt was wobbling. He put one finger in the air and came staggering over to the sidelines. It was really a bizarre sight. Matt seemed to be signaling "we're No. 1," but I know his head felt like No. 2. On the sideline the doctor determined that Matt had broken a front tooth off right at the gum line—and he also had a concussion. He was sitting there on the bench with a towel over his head, looking terribly battered. I limped over to him and tried to console him. Roy and Fran came over and asked what was Matt's injury. I said he hit his head. Francis looked at me, one of those heat-of-battle looks, because all three of us now, Francis, Matt and myself, were beat up. And Francis said, "Hell, he's all right."

I had to smile inwardly hearing that. Ballplayers, like coaches,

152

develop skill at diagnosing their teammates, and I'm no different.

The one guy who seems never to give a diagnosis is the only playing doctor on the team, Fred Cox, a chiropractor.

The fans mobbed the field when it was over, and there were so many bare backs and bare chests in the balmy weather that it resembled a college riot. As I was struggling across the field I caught Kenny Houston, who had his head down. Kenny is a good friend of mine who's been involved in fellowship work for years. Here was a man who had just experienced an awful day in his competitive life, losing a playoff game that might be one of his last chances to reach the Super Bowl. Yet when he saw me his thoughts were only for me. "What happened to you?" he asked. I told him, and he said he wished I would heal for next Sunday and that God would bless me.

I relate this because I don't think fans are aware that rival players are capable of that kind of gratitude right after a very bitter experience. And I think a stronger force is at work there than simple sportsmanship.

A few hours later I watched New England, on the verge of beating Oakland, and having outplayed the Raiders all afternoon, blow the playoff game on its own mistakes and penalty calls in the last quarter. I remembered our playoff game against Dallas a year ago, and I knew exactly what was gnawing at the brains and guts of the New England players as they stood hopelessly on the sideline with the clock ticking out.

Oakland was not impressive. I was certain they would have to play Pittsburgh in their conference championship game. And I was positive that Oakland a week from now would regret having beaten Cincinnati at the end of the regular season and forced itself to play Pittsburgh for the right to be in the Super Bowl.

I thought Pittsburgh would obliterate Oakland. That would mean, assuming we won a conference title as we expected to, that we would face the toughest team imaginable in the Super Bowl—Pittsburgh.

And on that day, I was certain, Oakland would be snorting out its regrets.

12

The Los Angeles Rams rolled into the National Football Conference title game in Minnesota with their usual complement of quality football players on the field and the familiar cast of subsidiary flakes and Wilshire Boulevard dynamos in the wings.

One of the team's physicians joined the athletes in a Christmas Day practice at Metropolitan Stadium, wearing shorts and t-shirt in the subfreezing weather. A fitness freak in his late forties, he was thumbing his nose at the Minnesota weather and Father Time. A printed announcement on the back of his t-shirt read: "F..K 50."

Francis Tarkenton arrived early for the Viking practice in order to exchange amenities with his old crony Fred Dryer, the one-time hippie blitzer. Tarkenton scanned the message on the physician's shirt and observed, "I'm glad Jeff Siemon's not here. That's his number. It's a terrible thing to tell Jeff."

Observing the Rams' simultaneous struggles to catch the ball and avoid frostbite, Carroll Rosenbloom prowled the sidelines as the Rams' boisterous grand marshal. He cursed the weather amiably and intensified the psychological warfare of playoff week by switching to an attack of generosity. "If the Minnesota legislature ever approves a domed stadium for this place," he said, "Carroll Rosenbloom pledges to make the first $1,000 payment." A bystander expressed hope that the weather might turn warmer, reminding Rosenbloom that the Vikings and the Redskins had played in 45-degree weather a week before.

"If it's 45 degrees for our game," Rosenbloom vowed, "I will stand in midfield and kiss the Vikings' mascot on the horns."

He said he would go further than that.

"If it's more than 45 degrees," he said, "I'll make an even more spectacular display of my gratitude."

One of the virtues of any championship football game is that it provides a merciful relief from the weeklong discharge of hot air that is mandatory on such occasions. The competition to produce the most imaginative b.s. is usually ferocious. One of the favorites for the title, unindoctrinated fans might be surprised to learn, is Bud Grant.

Even admirers of his craft admit that Grant does not appear to be tailored for the part. Outwardly he has all the melodramatic qualities of a sitting Buddha. This non-electrifying appearance, however, cloaks an agitator's soul and a rebel's heart.

Grant has been sniping at Rozelle's fortress for years, accusing it of needless interference in the affairs of football coaches. Grant is also fond of depicting the NFL office as a welfare board for incompetent officials and a casting agency for stage-struck league publicists.

Rozelle ignores some of Grant's zingers. Some of them he recognizes with a calm response here or a $1,000 fine there. Despite a stoutly earned reputation for thrift, Grant does not seem intimidated by either.

Five days before the Vikings-Rams game, Grant declared he was offended by a league decision requiring the Rams to fly into Minnesota on Christmas Eve. The NFL was a Scrooge. Grant wore his traditional long face in mourning, extending to Chuck Knox of the Rams his fraternal sympathies.

"It's a typical league operation," Grant said. "There's no rea-

155

son why a team has to leave home that early except that it's somewhere in the rules and the only justification there is for it is that it's always been done that way. I can't see one other excuse for it.

"Maybe it made sense when they had trains back in the 1940s," he said, "but it makes no sense now."

Trains, the NFL's Jim Kensil observed later, happened to be more reliable than planes, oddly enough. They were rarely socked in by fog and almost never got rerouted from Minneapolis to Dallas because of snowstorms. "But now we travel by plane, and the idea of requiring the team to be in Minneapolis on Friday night for a Sunday game is just to be sure we have a ball game."

Meteorologists would verify, Grant contended, that visibility at the Minneapolis–St. Paul International Airport averaged out a lot better than in Los Angeles.

Kensil congratulated the Minneapolis–St. Paul International Airport. But, he said, the Rams' early arrival eased the risk of transport delays, "and we certainly wouldn't want a ballclub showing up at 1 P.M. the day of the game."

By coincidence this was almost the exact hour at which Grant himself had brought his football team into Detroit three months earlier to force a half hour delay in the game's start.

"The trouble with the NFL operation out of New York," Grant said, "is that there is a lot of non-intelligence represented there. The qualification for a job is how well the guy does in pleasing Rozelle. I see one of the things they've scheduled for Christmas Day is a press conference."

One of the things Grant scheduled for Christmas Day was a workout.

None of the ball players filed a grievance petition. Christmas Day was, after all, one day before the ball game. The Rams did not seem overcome by gratitude for Grant's intervention.

"We always fly into the game site two days before the game," one of their officials said. "We did it in Minneapolis three months ago. We're not mad at anybody except the weather bureau."

The weather bureau earned the Rams' disapproval by forecasting zero temperatures or worse the morning of the game.

The Jeff Siemon vigil, in the meantime, was well under way. It involved Jeff Siemon, the Viking trainer, doctor, Bud Grant and, more than casually, 42 other ball players. An experienced middle linebacker—the hinge of the defense—was one player who occupied a nearly irreplaceable status for a title game.

From Jeff Siemon's journal

Tuesday, December 21   Nothing on television Sunday was a surprise. Pittsburgh obliterated Baltimore and Los Angeles beat Dallas. Pittsburgh took Baltimore apart from one end of the field to another. The Steelers are still the toughest football team in the NFL, as far as I'm concerned, and I think it's just a matter of time until Oakland regrets beating Cincinnati in that game near the end of the season.

Los Angeles' defensive power kept Dallas stymied most of the game. Roger Staubach played poorly, out of character for him, and he couldn't hit his receivers even when they were open. He's been a great quarterback and will be again. Maybe that thumb injury has bothered him more than he's said. Anyhow, I was secretly hoping Dallas would win, for selfish reasons. The Dallas offense hasn't been playing well and they can't seem to untrack their running game. They would have been easier for us in the playoffs.

I spent all day yesterday in the training room on every contraption Zamberletti could find. I don't know how much good they'll do. There's no replacing the natural healing process. What you try to do with Fred's treatment is to speed up the process.

Dr. Harry P. (for Psychotherapist) Grant was heavily engaged at this time trying to speed the process himself. On his weekly Monday night television show the question of Jeff Siemon's calf injury was brought up. Grant's dossiers have characterized Sie-

157

mon as a stubborn patient who insists on deciding for himself his own readiness for combat. It is a kind of independence that worries some coaches and enrages others. Grant is too secure for the one and too civilized for the other. He thought his TV show was an appropriate time, however, to practice some creative medicine, also called the power of suggestion, also called a word to the wise.

From Jeff Siemon's journal

Tuesday, December 21   Bud on his show Monday night was assessing our injury situation, and he compared mine with the one Mick Tingelhooff had years ago. Bud informed his audience (which naturally included me) that Mick was able to play in one week. I'm still not convinced Mick and I had the same kind of injury, but Bud is. I don't know whether he's doing it for psychological reasons, but the effect right now—if I have any accurate knowledge of the patient's state of mind—is just the opposite of what the psychologist wanted. I've got a feeling the whole week is going to be like this. It ought to be a carnival when the newspapermen and TV commentators all jump in with their own green smocks. I've always prided myself in playing with injuries that would keep the average guy out of the lineup. In five years I've missed one game, in a special team role my rookie year. I've played with injuries my whole career but I get the feeling, and it hurts, that some don't believe I would do absolutely anything in my power, suffer any kind of pain, to help the team.

Wednesday, December 22   There are more advisers than I imagined. I'm getting calls from fellow Christians, fans and a couple of faith healers. I feel I could make a difference in this game; not a crucial one perhaps, but I want to play in it badly. Still, the way I am now, I would be no help at all to the team, and it's impossible to know how strong my leg will be on Sunday.

I got my mind off my troubles by watching film and getting involved in our game plan. Of all the film available on the Rams the most important was our own, the game we played them in September. The Rams have a play we call a 35 and 35 cutback, which is run out of the flanker right formation. They ran that play seventeen times! One play represented one-fourth of their whole offense and one-third of their running offense. To that you could add their 34 to the other side, which they ran six or seven times. This means that one basic play made up one-half of their offense on the ground.

So when you prepare a defense for the Rams' running game, your homework is not going to keep you up past midnight. But it's not the planning for those big bruisers that occupies you; it's stopping them. They'll use most of the same offense because they've had success with it. And they aren't going to try to win an NFC title game on tricky offenses with that kind of power and with a rookie, Pat Haden, playing quarterback.

I never liked the Rams. I don't mean I have any strong animosity toward all their people, or even toward most of them. I grew up in Bakersfield, where most of the football fans were obnoxious Rams rooters. I wasn't. I think that now, knowing what I know as a player, I like them even less. The Rams generally have had some talkative people on their team. Because of the exposure they get Los Angeles football players often tend to be pampered people. It was very much the case at USC and to a lesser extent at UCLA when I was in school. The Rams are part of the tradition.

Isaiah Robertson, their linebacker, was talking in an interview after the Rams beat Dallas. He said very few people could run on the Rams with much success, the exceptions being Walter Payton and O. J. Simpson. Somebody asked what about Chuck Foreman. He indicated arrogantly that he would answer that question the following week. He went on and on, and basically he is a very extroverted type, which just doesn't happen to be my favorite type on a football team. It doesn't mean any personal vendetta Sunday—assuming I play, which is a lot to assume right now.

Our small prayer group met for perhaps the last time this season, and it was an uplifting time because we could all see specific answers to prayers we had brought before God. One answer concerned Amos Martin's wife, Edie. She had a history of thyroid problems.

Some of the thyroid was removed in an operation several years ago. She has a tendency to be nervous and, because her system is running so fast, she is tired at night. A number of doctors had told her there was nothing much that could be done. We prayed for her and for some solution.

I remembered my dad did his residency in the Mayo Clinic, in Rochester, Minnesota, and I asked if he might inquire. He called a friend and got an appointment for Edie. Pam Krause, however, arranged a medical appointment at Mayo that was better for the Martins' schedule. The doctors found that indeed there was something that could be done. They operated. It was a success. It was a direct answer to prayer. I believe God does honor consistent prayer.

On Thursday, three days before the game, Harry P. Grant circulated among reporters the gloomy forecast that Jeff Siemon did not seem to be responding and might very well not be ready to play the most important game of his season.

From Jeff Siemon's journal

Thursday, December 23   Bud was coming into the training room earlier in the week to look at the casualties. Tarkenton was there too, having his knee tended to. Bud doesn't say anything. He looks around. I don't know. Sometimes it's hard to read the look on his face, to know whether he's silently chiding or what. I'm sure he's concerned, but the last couple of days he hasn't been around. Maybe it means he's given up on Siemon's playing middle linebacker. Given Bud's rigid formula about practice, I'm sure I won't start Sunday. I've already missed four days. I just can't run. If you can't run you can't play. It's really a miserable feeling, knowing how important the game is to the team and the fans and realizing you might not be able to do it.

You fight guilt feelings. You know that they don't make sense and that they needlessly burden you. But it's almost impossible to avoid feeling that you're letting somebody down. I thought I might get some relief by going to a shop to get something for my wife for

Christmas. At least ten people must have asked if I was going to be able to play. They seemed genuinely sympathetic. The phone was ringing at home all night. Friends, writers, Dad—all with the same question.

Friday, December 24   It may have been the most frustrating day of my athletic career. Fred did one of the monumental tape jobs of the season. I shaved my leg from toe to crotch, and he began taping my foot and ended up in my upper thigh, trying to keep the pressure off the calf muscle. On the field I tried to run, but I felt the pain shooting from the lower part of my calf to the hamstring attachment. It looked like the finish for Sunday.

I did some other drills gingerly, because I didn't want to wreck any remote hope I had of playing. Seeing that, my tenderhearted teammates got out their spears. Krause is an ace in that department. He doesn't mean to be cruel, certainly, but the things Paul says for some reason sting, and on this day he really got to me.

The emotional tone for the game, generally, is good. The offense especially has generated enormous confidence. One of the big motivators is Chuck Goodrum, the offensive guard, who is almost unknown among the fans as a personality but comes to the park greatly excited every day. He'll need it against Larry Brooks.

Not all of the intramural shafts flung at Jeff Siemon wore pillow tips. Some of the club's veterans were frankly disdainful, convinced that Siemon was not driving himself to the outer limits of pain tolerance. He was therefore—by the hoary codes of the profession—coddling himself.

"I can't figure the guy out," one of them snapped to a teammate after the Christmas Eve workout. "The biggest game of the year and he's dragging his leg like it's going to fall off if somebody touches it. What the hell kind of injury do you risk? If you get rapped again, you get rapped. If it's a championship game, you play."

Siemon didn't hear it, but he would have been inhuman if he didn't realize there was talk like that.

161

From Jeff Siemon's journal

Sunday, December 26 I walked to the meeting room yesterday with a few teammates, thankful now that I didn't blow up two days ago when Ron Yary made a crack.

To another player he said something like, "Yeah, you and I and a couple of other guys are going to be playing our hearts out while Jeff is sitting on the bench." Something on that order, which Ron might have intended to be funny. Jokes are okay, but that was a bummer. My gut reaction was to smack Ron in the mouth. I controlled that. Most of all I wanted to get the next twenty-four hours over with. I was tired in the motel the night before the game, Christmas Night. I went to bed at 10:30, right after my roommate rolled over and went to sleep. It was a nice Christmas with the children and Dawn, and it's always great to see the kids' excitement.

My physical condition, I admit, took some of the joy out of the holiday. The locker room after practice was jammed with wiring and cameras for whatever post-game mood we are going to display. I had next to no hope of playing. As the hours peeled away I seemed more and more stigmatized by this noncombatant role. Halfway through breakfast another teammate leaned over and, displaying his typical flair for tact, said, "Siemon, while you are sitting on the bench and the rest of us are playing for the Super Bowl, I want you to split your bonus with us."

I thought he was talking about the money we would get for the playoff game, and I said I would be glad to if he would split his money with me for all the league games he has missed the last few years. I had missed one, and I know he had missed several.

He said no, he wasn't talking about the game check. He said he was talking about my bonus. Then it hit me that he meant the incentive clause I have in my contract that pays me $5,000 if we win the NFC championship game. I was amazed that he would even mention that with all the people around.

Sometime earlier he came to me to talk about signing a new contract, and he asked me candidly what my incentive clauses were.

162

I'm not one who is hush-hush on a contract, because that does more than anything else to injure the player's bargaining position. The more that players are quiet about their contracts, the easier it is for management to sign players to smaller contracts. I told my teammate exactly what my incentives were, but I did that in confidence. I did that not because I was worried about the information getting out, but because it isn't something you blurt out in front of your teammates. For him to make that statement about how he and the others were playing for the Super Bowl while I sat on the bench was the limit. It was about all I wanted to take.

After breakfast, as we were breaking up into offensive and defensive groups, I let him know that he was an obnoxious rear end. I said I didn't see how (No. 1) he could bring up that information I told him in confidence and (No. 2) that he had to be a callous person to continue bringing up the business about my not playing. There wasn't anybody who wanted to play more than I did, but nothing he or anybody else could say was going to change whether I played or not.

He dismissed it by saying he was sorry he said anything but that he thought I'd be more of a man if I accepted it. I wanted to ask him what "manhood" had to do with all of this, and just how do you define it in a situation like this. I'm convinced that being a man has nothing to do with being totally insensitive to the needs and feelings of others. It is the exact opposite of what being a man is all about.

I think society, and especially the type who too often speaks for athletic society, distorts the true concept of what a man is. As a result we have a needless amount of insensitivity masquerading as manhood.

The quilted battalions who watch football in Metropolitan Stadium in winter are the masked marvels of the NFL arenas. But they are nobody's clowns. The temperature was a little higher than advertised two days later, 10 above with a penetrating west wind that dropped the windchill to well below zero. In these conditions only the showboats among the tailgaters brought their vats and groaning boards. The rest of them stomped through the parking lots and concourses with breaths steaming. The arriving Rams observed the spectacle with unspoken curses and sudden depression.

Jack Youngblood was the bitterest of all. He was a tough guy, but he hated the cold. When you play college ball in Florida and pro ball in California, you might be excused for these hostilities. Freddie Dryer, his pass-rushing accomplice and the ranking satirist in the NFL, wanted to talk him out of it. Dryer had already tried to cleanse the ball game of what he considered unnatural grimness. From L.A. four days before he had disclosed the unleashing of a band of killer midgets who, he said, were programmed to ski over the Great Circle route direct into the Viking dressing room and administer a disabling enema to Tarkenton an hour before kickoff.

The midgets must have gotten caught in the usual Met Stadium traffic anarchy and never showed. Tarkenton informed Dryer in advance that he was unafraid, having taken some precautions which were never spelled out.

The Rams rushed onto the field for warmups *in shirtsleeves.* It was a form of graveyard whistling which impressed neither the Vikings, who wore standard jackets and were glad of it, nor the Rams, who almost petrified before they were waved into the locker room.

In the Viking brain trust, coach Jocko Nelson of the kicking teams and linebacker corps advised Grant he was ready to replace Jeff Siemon with Sammy Johnson as the deep blocker on the punting teams. Since Siemon was not starting at middle linebacker, Nelson reasoned, he probably was not in shape to handle the punting teams' assignments either.

Grant shook his head. "Keep Jeff on the punting team," he said. He wanted to get Jeff Siemon involved in the football game.

The blocking back's chores were routine; he hit anybody who threatened the punter and he hung back with the punter as dual safetyman. Even if his calf didn't improve, Grant reasoned, Siemon could handle that. And there was something about a big game, and adrenalin, and Fred Zamberletti's tape job . . .

From Jeff Siemon's journal

Sunday, December 26   Bud's breakfast message seemed to strike the right chord. He said we had a new dimension in our team this year, a new spirit, and it was real. He came right out and said we should go crazy on these guys.

Before that I had spent a little time in my room, asking the Lord that he might protect Amos and give him a special kind of ability to play to his capacity. I knew Amos preferred to play the outside. He was a middle linebacker out of necessity. The need had presented itself. I asked that the game might be a confidence builder for Amos. He needs this one big game, I think, to turn the corner in his career.

I went over to the training quarters early to put my leg in the whirlpool. While there I asked Lannin for an extensive Novocaine injection. He turned that down, and Zamberletti seconded him. Lannin said he didn't think it would do any good. And it's no secret that NFL clubs are afraid now of lawsuits growing out of the use of Novocaine. Also, Lannin has believed for a long time that for certain kinds of injuries pain is the body's best defense: It tells you of possible disaster ahead. Drugs remove that defense.

I was going to go the limit, though, to try to get myself into the game. This was perhaps the last championship game I would play in, and I knew that injecting into a muscle was not nearly as serious as injecting into a joint. There isn't much permanent damage you can do the muscle if it takes another bad blow. It would heal. Deadening a joint, and thereby exposing it to aggravated injury, can result in lasting harm and could conceivably cripple a person for life. I faced no such risk. I just wanted to do everything I could to play. Lannin wouldn't listen.

We couldn't believe the Rams without their warmup jackets. The wind made it numbing cold. I looked at some of the Rams as they took their turn in passing drill. They were going to play, all right, but they'd rather not.

Zamberletti had taped me before most of the guys came in. It was one of those tremendously elaborate tape jobs, and the stuff seemed to weigh ten pounds. But it made me feel pretty secure. And I found to my great amazement and satisfaction when I warmed up that I had pretty good movement from left to right, and not bad backpeddling. Straight ahead I was greatly restricted. And I wasn't going to scare anybody with my blinding speed. But I felt suddenly optimistic.

The guys were getting their pads on for the opening kickoff, and I caught Bud's eye as I walked by. He asked me how it felt. I told him. He said, "We may need you in there." I said I would like to see if I could go. He said it's not worth going in there if you can't play, and I said I understood that.

Bud knew that I wouldn't go in there to make a melodramatic appearance for the benefit of the fans or even the players if it meant jeopardizing the team's chances. I think most good professionals would think that way. In a sense I was hoping a situation wouldn't occur where I had to go in. It would have meant the Rams were moving the ball.

But that was a lofty thought that really didn't linger long. I wanted to play; it didn't really matter about the circumstances. The adrenalin had something to do with it. So did the championship game, Fred's taping skills, and maybe just the sounds of the stadium and the thrill that comes with being a participant in all that. Ed White was right. When the vibrations are right, your body just lifts you out of pain.

If the body juices churned in Siemon, they were equally active in the Rams' offensive team. The Viking prognosis was perfect. The Rams were going to try to storm them with Lawrence McCutcheon and John Cappelletti behind that gargantuan front. There was no deviation for the Rams. They came early. Neither the cold, the wind nor the Viking defensive line created any real impediment. The Rams' ground game moved with the unscenic efficiency of a sausage grinder, and it reached the Viking 1-yard line, which seemed an immense relief to the Viking defense.

It was a part of the world that had been the Vikings' sanctuary all season. Put them on the 1-yard line and they felt instantly secure and faintly invincible. It was an attitude that seemed to

166

infect the fans. The Rams were amazed to reach the Viking 1-yard line and to hear some of the front seat occupants beyond the end zone break into cheers.

On third down Pat Haden drove for the end zone. Wally Hilgenberg flung himself above Alan Page, Carl Eller and Doug Sutherland, who had burrowed into the Ram offensive line to fight for a standoff—which amounts to a victory for the defense when it is anchored on the goal line. The Rams howled that Haden was in the end zone.

The officials placed the ball three inches from the goal line.

The Rams' Chuck Knox, recalling his team's ghastly experiences on the goal line in Minnesota in September, waved in kicker Tom Dempsey. From the moment the Rams penetrated close to the Viking goal line it was clear that only some extraordinary act could prevent a touchdown. Such a deed was now furnished by Chuck Knox, who opted for three points from the three-inch line in the first quarter of a title game in which a strong early lead seemed crucial.

Fifteen seconds later the strong early lead was duly established.

And the Vikings had it.

Chuck Knox chose to heed one of football's shaggiest axioms: When you're on the goal line, don't come away empty-handed. It might have been a percentage decision, and Knox is an abundantly respected coach. But there was something about the moment that seemed to demand more—the largeness of it, the Rams' history of title game failure, the emotional and physical surge that brought the team to within three inches of a very significant goal.

One other axiom hovered over the Rams' decision, scarcely observed: There are worse things than coming away empty-handed.

They came away trailing, 7–0. Nate Allen, his furies undiminished on the kicking teams despite the loss of his cornerback job to Bobby Bryant, hurled himself toward Dempsey off the right corner. Diving, he blocked the ball with his hands. It caromed upfield and into the hands of Bobby Bryant, who sped 90 yards into the Rams' end zone.

Turning, Bryant smiled, held the ball in one hand and, as unobtrusively as you can in front of 40 or 50 million people, blew a kiss to his wife at the far end of the stadium.

It was the equivalent of a 14-point play: the touchdown the Rams didn't score plus the one the Vikings did. The Rams never completely recovered.

They rallied magnificently in the second half when, trailing 17–0, they scored 13 points and came within range of the winning touchdown in the final three minutes. They did all this in weather that bullied them and against halftime odds that would never have been seriously calculated in Las Vegas.

They got to the Viking 39. A blown extra point after their second touchdown altered their strategy from what it certainly would have been. From the 39 they would normally have mauled the tiring Minnesota front with Cappelletti and McCutcheon. A field goal would have sent the game into overtime. But, looking at a 4-point deficit, they couldn't spare the time on their running game. Young Haden threw on first down, on second and on third.

But the team that would be derided again two weeks later as the one that couldn't win the big ones produced the people who could. The money wasn't quite as big as it would be in Pasadena, but there really isn't much preoccupation with money on the line of scrimmage on fourth and ten of an NFC title game. What there is, primarily, is a collision of twenty-two desperate men.

Nate Wright, who was burned in the final minute by Dallas almost a year ago to the day, covered Harold Jackson on the first play. Haden's long throw fell incomplete. On second down Haden sent Ron Jessie one-on-one against Bryant. The strategy worked. Bryant found himself alone on Jessie, but he broke up the pass. On third down Jim Marshall and Carl Eller blew past the Rams' protection and disorganized Haden's rhythm, forcing the young quarterback to throw hurriedly to Cappelletti. The ball hit the ground.

Fourth and ten. Grant and Neill Armstrong conferred. Haden was throwing quickly when pressured. He would probably go deep to Jackson or Jessie. If the Vikings blitzed, sending Matt Blair and Hilgenberg against the quarterback along with the four rushing linemen, Jackson and Jessie were certain to be running one-on-one against Bryant and Nate Wright.

It would match two of the finest and fastest receivers in pro football against the unaided cornerbacks.

Armstrong ordered the blitz.

Hilgenberg and Blair charged with the Viking line at the snap. Spotting the blitz, Haden called the deep pattern, exactly as Tarkenton would have done. Jackson and Jessie bolted down the sidelines and cut. Haden threw quickly to Jessie crossing in the middle. The ball floated 40 yards. It was time enough for a cornerback with ten years experience in pro football to desert his man, although the manuals didn't tell him to, and sprint to the ball.

Bryant left Jackson and raced for the ball, which was spiraling toward Jessie a few yards from the goal line. Jessie was open. If he caught it, the Rams were going to score.

Bryant leaped.

And came down with the ball.

A minute later, on third down, Tarkenton carefully watched the Rams take his first, second and third receivers away from him when the Vikings needed to keep possession to protect the lead. With the rush closing, Tarkenton went to the fourth, Chuck Foreman.

"How's that," Tarkenton howled later, "for a fourth option. Chuck Foreman. The most valuable football player in the world. And he goes 57 yards, and then we score and we're home."

It finished, 24–13. In the middle of the frantic sideline embrace was Jeff Siemon, cold and grimy but exultant after an afternoon of linebacking.

From Jeff Siemon's journal

Sunday, December 26 We were leading, 10–0, but the Rams had shown a lot of power on the ground. I noticed on the punting team that my leg was relatively strong. As I was standing on the sideline near Bud Grant I leaned over and said, ''Bud, there's no way for me to know whether I can play unless I get in there and try to do something.'' He nodded and said he would talk to Neill. He suggested that if the Rams made another first down I should go in. They did, and I went in.

I guess every football player has an ego big enough to appreciate special attention. When I heard the fans shouting and applauding as I entered, I was stunned. It was one of the few times I had ever experienced a crowd's reaction to me personally in all my years in football. I knew their reaction was a positive thing that was directed toward me and not against Amos, who had played all right. And I got lucky. Mostly because I wasn't blocked very well, I made a couple very visible tackles in the first series I was in. I could have been coldly analytical and told myself that it was pure chance, making those tackles. But you're human. You get caught up in the emotion. It's a terrific feeling to actually be part of a championship team.

We didn't stop them every play by a long shot. The Rams are an immensely tough football team. I thought we had established supremacy with Chuck Foreman's 62-yard run and the subsequent touchdown for a 17–0 score. I can chide myself now for saying the Rams were pampered. I don't know whether they are. But they came back with great courage in the second half. And it all came down to that fourth and ten play on our 39 with three minutes to go.

I went over to the sideline to discuss it with Neill Armstrong. It got to whether we would use a four-man rush and our basic defense in that situation or blitz the two outside linebackers. Neill asked me what I'd like to do and I said it was his decision. He said he was leaning toward the blitz, and I said why not, it's a big-play call. Either you do it successfully or you lose the game. I thought it was the kind of hang-it-out call we needed. If the Rams made a first down, they had plenty of time to score; and if we blitzed, there was a real chance they were going to get it all on that play.

The blitz made Haden throw in a hurry. He got it out there, but with just enough loft so that Bobby Bryant was able to make that tremendous play to intercept. I guess you have to be a professional football player to appreciate what he did. When you're one-on-one against a great receiver like Harold Jackson, *that is your play*. Jackson is all you're supposed to be thinking about. But Bryant had one eye on Jackson and one eye on the quarterback. He's one of the finest big-play football players I've ever seen. He's a ball player who creates the situation for a big play. So he barrelled over as soon as he saw Haden release the ball to Jessie. And then he had to time his jump. I don't think most of the crowd or the television audience really recognized all of the experience, the finesse, the timing and the guts that went into making a play like that.

And then, a few minutes later, there was Tarkenton, who had been struggling all day like most of us—well, it just wasn't one of his better games. But on the one down when all of his skills and mental toughness were needed most, he delivered. That ball he threw to Foreman after seeing his first three receivers covered was one of the greatest clutch passes he or any other quarterback will throw. I spent some time with him in the training room during the week. I know his leg wasn't sound, and it had to affect his maneuverability and therefore his passing performance. But he had that ball right on Foreman's hands on third down—and never mind the windchill factor.

I had a little time to reflect after the game when the mob scene in the dressing room had subsided. I think the closeness you build with your teammates, the sharing of the struggle and those unforgettable flights of jubilation forty-three people take together in victory —or the despondency they shoulder together in defeat—those are the things that make playing worthwhile in an enduring sense. The belief; the oneness, even if it may be transitory.

I looked over to Carl Eller's locker, where Moose was slowly putting on his tie. I don't know anybody who can make the kind of long-term production out of knotting a tie that Moose can. And I don't know many people—any, really—that I respect more on this team.

In the Rams game, while a lot of people played well (including the Rams, of course), Bobby Bryant and Carl Eller were the guys for the Vikings. Moose was everywhere making tackles. I have played with him for five years, and I can't think of a game where he was better. And here was Carl Eller, twelve years in the league, after absorbing the criticism he did during the season. Yet he was capable in a team crisis of producing a game like that. He had played on the same level the week before, in the playoff game with Washington. What was it Bud said about Moose? When his opponent is good enough or the game is big enough, Eller will give it his undivided attention.

I know it's true. He played the same kind of game last year in the playoffs against Dallas. I think he made ten tackles and three quarterback sacks on Roger Staubach—against one of the finest offensive linemen in modern pro history, Rayfield Wright.

I just wanted to go over to Moose, shake his hand, and tell him how proud I was to be playing with him on the Minnesota Vikings.

They nearly lost a few getting to the locker room. By the hundreds the tribes charged onto the field from the grandstands, engulfing the players, ambushing the goalposts.

"If we had to play our fans all afternoon instead of the Rams," a shaken Ed White said afterward, "we might not have made it. Coming off the field was like fighting your way through a thousand linebackers. We won the war and nearly got killed enjoying the peace. It was beautiful, but it was brutal. You can't blame the fans for wanting to celebrate, but I wish they would have done it in the parking lot. It wasn't their beating on our heads that bothered the ball players. It was their breath that almost knocked us over."

Maybe they should have started some of the fans against Oakland two weeks later.

13

The Man from Mars disgorged a huge mushroom of cigar smoke which temporarily eclipsed him as a heavenly body.

Dispersing slowly, it revealed to the gaping earthlings gathered around the table a shiny, spherical object. On closer observation it turned out to be Otis Sistrunk's hairless head.

The heavenly body spoke.

"Those Vikings are fine, God-fearin' fellas," he said. "It would be nice if they could win a Super Bowl game, real nice. That team has so much, but it has misfortune. I know the first thing you fellas from the press want to know is what kind of misfortune. I'll tell you: The Vikings' misfortune is they got to play the Oakland Raiders. I wish there was some comfort I could give to the Vikings, but there ain't. People ask me, 'how can you beat Francis Tarkenton and the Vikings with a three-man line,' and I say, man, we ain't got a three-man rush. We ain't got a four-man rush. What we got is an eleven-man rush. It may not show in the films, but it shows in our hearts."

He seemed saddened that the world had not recognized this cardiovascular truth, and he spoke with a sense of sincere regret that the Vikings themselves seemed unaware of the holocaust

ahead. His voice was gentle, totally devoid of threat or antago-
nism. It was tolerant and affable, qualities clearly much prized
at the University of Mars, which Alex Karras claimed was Otis'
alma mater. Karras' theory was inspired by Otis' magnificent
domed cranium and the absence of earthly college credits in
Sistrunk's transcripts. Yet Otis' benign dignity three days before
the Super Bowl seemed to reject all notions of belligerence
ascribed to visitors from the red planet. It obviously pained him
to be the carrier of bad news.

"If you've got an eleven-man rush in your heart," asked one
of Otis' interrogators archly, "does that mean Tarkenton will
need X rays to pick up your defensive calls?"

Otis made a large O with his bountiful lips and, lifting his eyes
to the ballroom ceiling, discharged another volley of fumes. In
volume and configuration it resembled the steam column of the
Wabash Cannonball running twenty minutes behind schedule.

"Man," he said, "we don't have any weaknesses. I just don't
want Francis to be surprised when he sees that. He's such a nice
fellow, real religious like, and a credit to the game. I don't want
to hurt him. I just want to bury him."

An Otis Sistrunk playing for anybody but the Oakland Raiders in 1976 would have been a violation of natural selection and
environmental law. The Raiders were the Allen's Alley of pro
football. They offered asylum and a chance for redemption (re-
spectability was optional) to the free-falling eccentrics and
roustabouts of football. Oh, certainly they had great football
players. But the Raider management did not insist on this as an
admission card because greatness could be acquired, Al Davis
maintained, through exposure to the Oakland system, of which
Al Davis, coincidentally, was the architect.

Davis was managing general partner. He brought to the job
studiously sharpened qualities of cunning and vengefulness. He
had the style of a bar fighter and a reputation for genius which
he had never strenuously denied. Rivals were afraid to deal
with Davis for the fundamental reason that they were almost
certain to lose. Further, they might not know for years what it

had cost them besides money. Davis appeared to be not only brilliant but innovative, a combination that terrifies most owners and executives in the jock industry. He was smart enough to draft Kenny Stabler, Gene Upshaw, Fred Biletnikoff, Jack Tatum, Phil Villapiano, Clarence Davis, John Vella, Art Shell, Dave Casper and all the other high-rounders. But he was also some kind of Devil's Island missionary, another odd administrative role from which most NFL executives shrink. Al Davis fervidly believed he could reclaim the wastrel spirits and abandoned headhunters who sought or were offered shelter under his roof.

None were so designated on the Oakland roster. "When you join the Raiders," said Gene Upshaw, the 260-pound guard and candidate attorney, "beautiful things happen to you. The past is forgotten. All we care about is what you do with the Raiders. They can tell all the jokes they want about Oakland running a halfway house or a detention home. We're champions. Anybody got any more jokes?"

The congregation suddenly ran out of funnies.

Upshaw, however, stepped into the breach himself. On the Raiders, even three days before the Super Bowl, solemnity is officially barred. Upshaw freely admitted that he might be the best offensive lineman in football. He thought it no more than appropriate.

"I don't apologize to say it," he confided, "but we've got a helluva bunch of linemen. In Oakland they pay their offensive line. Other guys run and pass, but tell me where Paul Revere would have been without the horse. The trouble was Revere got more ink than the horse, but with our outfit the horse might have been the one they wrote poems about. I'm going against Alan Page. Great football player. I've known him better than ten years. He claims I grab and hold. The only guy who grabs better is Alan Page. Watch him Sunday. He'll do that. I see Alan says he doesn't cheat in line play. He claims he's a moralistic player. We ain't going to church Sunday. We're going to the line of scrimmage in the Super Bowl. There's a difference. I'll tell you they can talk all they want about the Stablers and the Tarkentons, but it's the Upshaws and Pages who win the Super Bowls."

Or who, he added after a philosophical pause, lose it.

"The quarterback, he may be the Willie Shoemaker if you want to compare football with a horse race. Upshaw? He's Secretariat."

He paused again to examine the economic implications of such a role.

"I just wish," he said, "I had Secretariat's stud fees."

Upshaw's lament was greeted by generous expressions of sympathy.

If the Raiders offered a dias for such portfolioed executives as Upshaw, Stabler and Art Shell, they also granted a refuge for vagabonds like Sistrunk, Dave Rowe, John Matuszak, Errol Mann, Carl Garrett and Willie Hall. They took drifters who were shunned by other teams in pro football for disabilities that included high salaries, mutinous hearts, drug use and a tendency to shank 20-yard field goals in awkward situations. None of these vices was disqualifying if the applicant was big enough, fast enough, ornery enough or if the Raider's needs were desperate enough.

Davis thus sponsored a migration of forsaken souls, and for these John Madden functioned as a big-bellied Statue of Liberty. John offered solace and the strong possibility of playoff money as the prize for reformation. He was an excellent coach and a harassed wit whose personality was largely misread by television audiences. On television Madden gives you the impression that you are watching a car wash manager running a football team on his day off.

Few coaches in America anguish as frankly or as publicly as John Madden. Are the Raiders floundering, are the officials hopelessly inept, are the opponents conniving with the operator of the scoreboard clock? John Madden's pumpkin cheeks will tell you. He lifts a fleshy hand to brush back his distraught forelocks. His eyes contract. He scowls the scowl of a man not only wronged but mystified as to why he should be selected by a mindless fate. He turns to aides for some shaft of enlightenment. He shakes his massive head and resumes his sideline prowl.

The situation, his sympathizers explain, is temporary. It is nothing that cannot be relieved by another turn-in from Stabler to Biletnikoff.

Only such a man, the Raider adherents reasoned, a man rough, savvy, fallible and forgiving, could both absorb Al Davis and execute his will.

And such a man should therefore be the ideal coach to merge the Kenny Stablers and Gene Upshaws with the George Atkinsons and Skip Thomases. The Raider practices some days struck a tone halfway between meetings of the Bay Area Bolshevik Society and a Holy Rollers' reunion. Other days they resembled a seance. The young goliath, Charles Philyaw, once spent fifteen minutes in a film session before being overtaken by a discomforting thought. Philyaw is a defensive lineman. Everybody else in the room belonged to the offense.

The Raider roster appeared to draw equally from the ranks of the nation's college stars and the late Saturday night horror shows. It featured a Doctor Death playing cornerback, Skip Thomas, who in the midst of action was said to speak strange incantations that baffled enemy receivers and the Raider linebackers alike. Rivals maintained that George Atkinson, one of the safeties, played like the Godfather's oldest boy executing a contract. By way of denying it Atkinson filed a multi-million-dollar lawsuit against coach Chuck Noll of the Pittsburgh Steelers and an Oakland newspaper.

Nothing about the Raiders seemed normal. Their lightweight defensive backs hit harder than their defensive linemen. They ran to the left on offense where everybody else ran to the right. They had a six-foot-eight social commentator and comedian (Ted Hendricks) playing linebacker, a defensive end from another planet (Sistrunk), a defensive back who owns race horses (Atkinson), a left-handed quarterback in Stabler and a reputation for employing aggravated assault as a substitute for defense.

None of this distressed the Minnesota Vikings.

The Vikings were convinced almost by acclamation that Oakland was a football team they should beat in the Super Bowl—and probably by a substantial margin.

They thought Pittsburgh was the class of the AFC and believed the Steelers would have made it to the Super Bowl again if they hadn't lost Franco Harris for the AFC title game. They had no real esteem for the Oakland defense. They thought Villapiano was overrated, and they could foresee no defensive line made up of Otis Sistrunk, Dave Rowe and John Matuszak causing them much grief.

They looked at Matuszak especially with eagerness. As a Raider he may have undergone some kind of rebirth, which in itself is a memorable biological feat for a man six-foot-seven and 280 pounds. But he would not have passed through so many football organizations in the past three years if he had played the type of defense that matched his tape measurements. He was strong, of course, and adequate against running plays, but (the films suggested) he was a bearded marshmallow as a pass rusher. Rowe was another old retread, as large as Matuszak but not much more fearsome, and Otis Sistrunk simply proved that Martians might look normal after all but they still couldn't play the whole defensive line by themselves.

While making these judgments, the Minnesota Vikings carefully avoided any disrespect or hauteur. Wouldn't you, with the kind of Super Bowl record they brought into Pasadena? It was an assessment based on film and a casual study of the Raiders' recent history. Oakland wasn't playing a three-man line out of any fanatic devotion to it tactically or numerically. Three months ago injuries wiped them out on the defensive line. Art Thoms, Kelvin Korver, Horace Jones and Tony Cline all went down. Davis and Madden regrouped with the calculating gall of rum runners and decided the solution was Sistrunk, Rowe and Matuszak fronting four linebackers. Hendricks, Villapiano and Monte Johnson they had no hesitation about. Willie Hall, in the middle, was another reclamation project, this one salvaged from the Raiders' own reject pile of the year before.

He played so well it had to shake Al Davis' faith in his own brilliance for evicting Willie in the first place. Davis, however, survived this crisis in confidence without breaking stride. If you're so right so many times, is infallibility really important?

The Vikings couldn't suppress their excitement at the prospect of facing some of these doubtful prodigies. Mystic forces seemed to be at work for them this time, and they were wearing white horns and purple heads. The one team that alarmed them in the AFC, Pittsburgh, had disappeared. They were healthy and on an emotional flight. In all their years of winning football, they could not remember such unity of the clan or buoyancy of the soul. The Raiders were walking into the Super Bowl carnival for the first time and would have to absorb its assorted shocks. The Vikings had seen them all. There wasn't a stupid or loaded press conference question they hadn't heard, or a hotel lobby madhouse they had not escaped. They came to California with the controlled fever of the crusade, but they were immune to the gasses of the Super Bowl sideshow.

There was one other part of the Super Bowl XI equation that might have been written by Aesop rather than the publicists. The Minnesota Vikings, to their admirers at least, somehow represented the solid verities of professional football and the social order. They wore orthodox clothing, drove recognizable cars, did not consider signing a letter of intent for Mars, and were hardly ever accused of playing dirty football or owning racehorses.

The Oakland Raiders were the jivies, oddballs and reformed hooligans. They were great for television closeups with their beards and their voodoo signs. But in the highlight film at the Hall of Fame in Canton, who would you rather have, Doctor Death or Nate Wright?

Did the question really have to be answered?

From Jeff Siemon's journal

Thursday, January 6   The only bad part of getting into the Super Bowl is the ticket hassle. It was worse this time than ever. My ticket demands were incredible. Long-lost pals emerge from Australia; you discover relatives of relatives; a half dozen people have sons, daughters, mothers or fathers near death who may be magically cured if you can get them a couple of tickets for the Super Bowl in Pasadena. It must be a healing spa that can't be explained by medical science. I ordered 250 tickets, the maximum allowed any player by the Viking management. I heard of my playing buddies, though, who asked for a thousand.

The ticket manager tried to allocate the tickets roughly on the basis of need, seniority and, I suppose, the size of the guy's salary. The tickets cost me $20 apiece (the face value of the ticket). You can figure it out. Multiply 250 by $20 and you've got $5,000, to be deducted from your Super Bowl check. If your check turns out to be the losers' share, it will come to $7,500. When you subtract taxes, deductions and the cost of the tickets from the Super Bowl check, you are probably going to come in with a minus figure for the week —which is not a thrilling prospect at all. You will be repaid for some of those tickets, naturally; but it will depend on the arrangement, and you won't always be sure.

Day and night we were lobbied by scalpers who offered as much as $100 a ticket. So you had guys who had given five or ten tickets to friends suddenly kicking themselves for not setting them aside and making a quick $500 or more. A couple of people on the team sold huge blocks of tickets to travel agencies and tour promoters, for profits in the thousands. Most of us sold some, at least, to balance the ones we gave away. And then there were guys who ended up with practically nothing to give to friends—which underlines the inequality of the whole thing.

Where the system broke down was in the cases of players who had close ties in California but had only a handful of tickets, while others with no connections out there had hundreds of tickets. I know

I felt guilty myself. I couldn't fill all the requests I had from people in California, but when I got there and sold a few I noticed other players with more pressing needs than I had. I scrounged around trying to find a few tickets to help them out. It was a kind of hustling you really could have done without just a few days before a championship football game. But you can't feel very offended by it, either; I know people from two dozen other football teams who would dearly love to have that kind of problem the first week of January.

The usual Super Bowl song and dance surrounded you. There was an enormous outpouring of writers and photographers for our first practice at the Rams' training site in Long Beach. You also got a role in the flesh market when the players filed into the motel ballroom and sat around while reporters moved about the room examining targets of opportunity. But you don't really have much of an opportunity for deeper looks at football or the people in it at these sessions. There are time limits, mobs of people and somebody is always announcing that the bus is going to leave for the Raider motel in ten minutes. I don't find these gatherings especially dehumanizing, just not very productive.

In a way I envy Francis. He always draws reporters by the platoons, but he really seems to enjoy all the needling and the encounters, and he's better at it than anybody I've seen in this game.

First, maestro—they were advancing on Tarkenton with their deferential opening questions—can you give some broad overview of the forthcoming epic?

Tarkenton was prepared to be bold and assertive. Defiant? No, not quite. Confident? Yes, but something stronger. Arrogant? Ah, certainly. It is the maestro's latest posture. The successful quarterback, the quarterback in command, is arrogant. Three years ago Francis Tarkenton was just pretending. His glares lacked a certain quality of menace and retribution that made them believable on a Bobby Layne. If you spend thirteen years of your pro career being called the preacher's kid and the scrambler, it takes a while before the officials and linebackers believe you're now the Terrible Turk.

181

But in his grizzled late thirties, with his facial creases and drill sergeant's rhetoric, Tarkenton was credibly arrogant, all right, and sometimes he even believed it himself.

"The Vikings are on fire," he said. "We're obsessed. We can feel it. And we're going to win this thing."

Never, he said, had the Vikings fielded such a football team from the top to the forty-third man. They had never played or lived with such utter togetherness and happiness.

The prelude finished, the maestro removed his cloak as a revealer of truth and pretended to kick one of his interrogators in the testicles.

It was more or less an official announcement that the Super Bowl circus had opened with all trapezes flying, and the man in the center ring—by acclamation—was Francis Tarkenton. His first act was a 90-minute press conference, the longest conducted on the West Coast since Nikita Khrushchev's appearance, and one easily more crowded than Khrushchev's.

The object of most of his oratory was the stupidity of the sporting press, which he said he was prepared to forgive but which he felt a duty to expose. He did not wish it to be construed as a carpet-bombing attacking. Most of the ignorance, he said, was centered in L.A.

"I'll tell you what you guys lack," Tarkenton said. "You're bright and great company, but you don't know a damned thing about football. You pick an all-pro team, and here's a guy like Chuck Foreman. He gains a thousand yards, catches more than fifty passes, and he wins. But in Buffalo they count yards for the running back instead of winning, and when you have to pick a running back you look at the yardage totals, and O. J. beats out Chuck Foreman. You pick offensive linemen but you never see them. I couldn't pick an all-pro offensive line, and I've been playing in this league for sixteen years."

Having been exposed and flogged as imposters, the inquirers now asked the custodian of wisdom if he could help them foretell the winner of the football game a few days hence. No, not the winner, since he had already announced that; but rather, "how." How were the Vikings going to accomplish this grand deed that had eluded them with such determination for so many years?

Tarkenton now chose diplomacy, which may be inconsistent for an arrogant quarterback, but it may also explain why he was in his sixteenth year.

"The thing that may make this the most exciting Super Bowl of all is that you've got for the first time two great offenses on the field."

So it was going to be a high-scoring game.

"Not necessarily. You can make a lot of yards without scoring a lot. If I told you how we're going to win, you'd dump me flat and go over and talk to Tingelhoff. Loyalty. Don't you guys talk to me about loyalty."

Francis lifted his head and howled. It was good, professional comedy. Somebody from *Saturday Night* should have recorded it because it was better than the material they gave Tarkenton four weeks later.

You could identify them in the Viking hotel lobby by their unpolished shoes, their nicotine-flavored sports jackets and their habit of talking through their lips as though the bellhop worked for the IRS. They were ticket peddlers, sawdust-floor operatives in the middle of a chichi extravaganza. The ticket hustle made the carefully groomed NFL posture of decorum the most amusing hypocrisy of the whole show.

The Super Bowl ticket allocation is the world's most bizarre sweepstakes. It has a potential of 80,000 or 90,000 winners, depending on the number of seats in the stadium. Very few tickets ever wind up in the possession of the people to whom they are first sold. Today's Super Bowl ticket is primarily a negotiable bond. Some 30,000 of them were sold in 1976 to purchasers of Los Angeles Rams season tickets, an arrangement which stirred the civic-minded heart of Rams owner Carroll Rosenbloom. It also helped Rosenbloom sell Rams season tickets by giving the buyers the added inducement of a chance to buy

Super Bowl tickets. Were they excited by the prospects of seeing the Rams in the Super Bowl? Romanticists should lower their glistening eyes. What excited Rams customers was the prospect of scalping the Super Bowl tickets to travel agencies, airlines and red-eyed fanatics from the towns playing in the Super Bowl.

With 30,000 tickets committed to Rams customers, the league had to limit Oakland and Minnesota to 15,000 each because the other twenty-six clubs were allocated 1,000 apiece and 17,000 more went to Ford, Chrysler, the City of Pasadena, the television networks, the L.A. media and all those people who inflated the Goodyear blimp.

Did this mean that all of the tickets sold to Oakland and Minnesota season ticket holders launched these grateful people to Pasadena?

Blush once more, romanticists.

Thousands of them scalped their tickets. One ticket broker estimated that only 5,000 Viking fans actually used the tickets they bought. The most violent accusations of chiseling and larceny did not come from the left-behind fans, however. The real war involved chiselers vs. chiselers—the amateur scalpers vs. the professional scalpers.

Ernie the Ticket Tout complained acidly from a barstool in the South Coast Plaza, where the Vikings were lodged. Ernie needed a shave and shoe polish, but he needed mouthwash even more. Still, he was an acceptable guest on the fifteenth floor, where the Vikings hawked any fresh infusion of tickets. Ernie was identifiable as a ticket pusher because he kept his hands in his pockets a lot and swiveled his head instinctively at the passage of a Viking linebacker.

"The dummies are buying tickets for $100," he groaned. "Right now, four days before the game. They're afraid they're going to miss out on the event of the century, and they want to be able to tell every relative from the farm that they saw the Super Bowl. First of all, if it's like most Super Bowls they're going to be ashamed to admit they were there in the first place.

184

Second, you can come to Pasadena Sunday morning. You can take your time. You can go for a swim in the hotel pool the morning of the game. You can ride to the Rose Bowl and you can buy a ticket for $2 a half hour before the game. The $100 dummies have been in their seats for two hours, and your seat will be better than theirs.

"Me, I give people a fair deal. I take care of friends. I got to make a profit. There's nothing wrong with $50, maybe $60 for a $20 ticket. I call that being a capitalist. I call $100 being a hog. The hogs go to the slaughterhouse. It's something I always say, Why be a hog? Why be a dummy? The dummies that are selling against me are gonna keep those tickets till too late, then they're gonna sell them for $2 a half hour before the game."

Ernie was 50 percent wrong.

You could buy a Super Bowl ticket thirty minutes before kickoff for $1.

Unawed by the figures being shopped around by the ticket brokers, NBC swept into the Super Bowl scene with its own dazzling mathematics. It had imported, NBC announced, twenty-one color cameras for Sunday's game—just one shy of a color camera for every player on the field. Of these, seven would be assigned to the $20,000 think tank specially constructed for the network's Grandstand Show, where Francis Tarkenton would be able to make taped appearances on leave from the Viking huddle. To prevent any lingering suspicion that it was neglecting its guests, NBC also organized a special breakfast and cocktail party for sponsors and TV personnel, at a cost of $60,000.

Just as considerate, the NFL produced a $75,000 fiesta at the Pasadena civic center the Friday night before the game. It was a form of convalescence for 2,500 people who had already fought their way through the league's free press breakfasts and luncheons earlier in the week.

The Mexican party revealed the NFL at its finest when the chips were on the line. Its Super Bowl records threatened by

NBC's cocktail party and breakfast, the NFL reached splendid heights by unleashing 15,000 tacos, enchiladas and tortillas, 10,-000 pieces of shrimp, 60 gallons of chili, 1,000 quarts of booze, two bands, 25 security officers and four medical doctors to handle the most dedicated convalescent cases.

Among the special guests was Harry P. Grant, who had spent a fair amount of his podium time denouncing the NFL for sideshow pre-game parties. He found it all very gala, so much so that he was late for the hotel bus returning the Viking contingent to Costa Mesa. It gave him two jewels on a rare triple crown of the Super Bowl. He was also twenty-five minutes late by helicopter for the league's special pre-game press conference earlier in the day. "If Grant shows up late for the Super Bowl," an NFL aide clucked, "he's got his choice of alibis—heartburn or airsickness."

Nobody was going to accuse John Madden of overcoaching in the Super Bowl. The Vikings expected him to run to the left? Beautiful. Why be contrary? The Raiders would run to the left. They always did. They had Art Shell at 300 pounds and Gene Upshaw's 270 pounds over there, and when Dave Casper lined up beside them they had another 240 pounds from the tight end.

The Vikings would try to match them with Jim Marshall, Alan Page and Wally Hilgenberg. Siemon would overshift there, but who didn't? Marshall was always announced at 230 pounds. Nobody in the NFL believed it in December and January, when he was usually down to 218 pounds—approximately two pounds more than he weighed for Super Bowl XI. He was also announced as thirty-nine years of age, which was accurate. Shell was more than 80 pounds heavier, ten years younger and an all-pro.

Page might have helped under normal conditions, but Upshaw wasn't normal. He outweighed Page by more than 30 pounds and was, by his own admission, probably the best offensive lineman on earth. Hilgenberg was belligerent and tough but old and light, which made Wally's attributes a sort of stand-off.

When they had to pass, or wanted to, the Raiders were going to let Snake Stabler loiter around 10 yards behind Shell, Upshaw, Dave Dalby and John Vella, and throw darts to Fred Biletnikoff and Casper. If the Raiders were pressed, he would throw 60 yards to Cliff Branch. It didn't matter much to John Madden or the Raiders—any way the Vikings wanted to go.

Defensively, it was decided unanimously by the Raider high command that Oakland could win the Super Bowl by playing a routine Oakland game. Let the Vikings snicker about the three-man front of Matuszak, Rowe and Sistrunk. They could handle the Vikings offensive line. The four linebackers and headchopping defensive backs would smother Tarkenton's long floaters, his sideline throws to White and Rashad and his curls to Voigt. They weren't worried about the beanbag passes.

As a matter of plain truth, they didn't worry much about anything. The Las Vegas line read 5 points for Oakland a day before the game, and the Raiders were stunned that the bookies were so timid.

From Jeff Siemon's journal

Sunday, January 9 The internal pressures of the game never revealed themselves in our practices. We had uniformly good practices, I thought, despite the damp weather and slow field at Long Beach. We heard the Raiders were running into impossible practice conditions, and here again everything seemed fated for us. We worked Saturday morning at a Pasadena high school field because the Rose Bowl turf was softened by the soaking rain. The bystander couldn't have imagined this team getting ready for the biggest football game of the year. There was a lot of goofing around and razzing —a typical Saturday morning practice, actually. It served as a release from the inside pressures I mentioned. I'd be amazed if it wasn't the same for Oakland.

We spent Saturday night at the Huntington in Pasadena. It's one of the grand old hotels of the West Coast, a showpiece when it was built in the early 1900s. The grounds are still lovely and the lobby and dining rooms, the halls and the vestibules still have grace and character. But there's only so much you can do to restore a seventy-year-old hotel. The rooms, frankly, were decrepit—and a little amusing to a bunch of athletic globetrotters who have seen the most luxurious modern hotels.

We had the best chapel turnout of the year last night. There were faces there that seldom materialized during our weekend meetings. I was pleased and thankful. What was the old army maxim? There are no atheists in foxholes. Or, I might add, on the night before the Super Bowl.

At breakfast today we heard that Jeff Wright had thrown out his knee going to the bathroom sometime after midnight. Doc Lannin and Fred Zamberletti were called in and treated it. For hours it looked as though Jeff might be out of it. But the thing popped back in just a couple of hours before we headed for the Rose Bowl. Just one more omen.

The weather was a little warm but almost perfect. I didn't really know what that meant for a team that had won most of its big games in below-freezing temperatures, but I'll take 60 degrees. It was just a few minutes by bus. Tark and Hilgenberg were wisecracking at the rear. Situation normal. We had feared a traffic jam, but so had about 100,000 other people.

The Rose Bowl's concourses and ramps were jammed when we drove up. There was an effigy twisting in the breeze, wearing a purple helmet and a number 10 jersey. If Tarkenton saw it, he paid no attention. The police and security people formed a corridor for us through the curious and yelling fans. Ball players always look their sternest at this moment, almost comically grim. You don't really want to get involved with the crowds. They may be good people, but they move in another orbit socially. A football game is a spectacle, and the players are the ones on exhibit. Because of that you constrict into your own world. Let the fans yell and boo and raise the roof; they have an entirely different kind of investment in the afternoon. They want thrills, winning, something to take home. But the ball players relate to ball players. That is why, when the crowd pours onto the field after the game to congratulate the players, you sometimes get actual fights between players and fans. The players don't want to be mauled or handled; the field is the ball players' preserve, and the fans belong in the grandstands. But no ball player should forget, either, that the fans make the whole show go.

The Super Bowl is a different, bigger, grander kind of game. There is no use trying to kid yourself about that. No matter how experienced you are, the realization of the size of it starts to take hold of you during your warmups and the locker room vigil. It was even bigger for us than it was for Oakland; you couldn't deny that, either. This was Super Bowl Four for the Minnesota Vikings. It was the first for Oakland in ten years, and it was a new experience for most of them. We speculated privately in the week leading up to the game about what the public would say if the Minnesota Vikings lost their fourth Super Bowl. So, psychologically, we had a huge stake in this —to avoid ridicule, if nothing else.

Sometimes that can be a big motivation, but it wasn't the biggest. We had been through a strange, sometimes exasperating season. Yet in December it was a very uplifting season. I'm not a hotbreath kind of emotional player, but I couldn't agree with Foreman more. We had built something different and closer in the past few months. And right now you could see it in the faces of the players. The unity and the fever were real. I've never been part of a locker room scene like the one before this game.

McNeill had brought his tape recorder. When we installed the stereo at the Met it had both turntable and tape units; after awhile some of the guys began bringing tape recorders and playing them on buses, planes and in hotel rooms. Fred had one album he played over and over again, and he put it on before the Super Bowl. It was from the soundtrack of *Car Wash,* a movie that had shown in the Twin Cities. I don't know the name of the song or whether it has words, but it has a special beat to it, and you could feel the emotion rising. We were ready in full battle dress and the adrenalin was surging. It was primitive and pretty wild. You felt a brotherhood and a shared strength that was electrifying. People started clapping their hands and stomping their feet to the beat of the music. It was tribal and ritualistic, but it was electrifying. The eyes got bigger and the hands became sweaty. I never thought I'd be part of a psyching-up quite like that. It seemed to take control of you.

And then we went out into the corridor and onto the field, and the whole pageant hit you in the face. Chanting, roaring, the banners waving—it was like those massive German political rallies of the 1930s I remembered from old newsreels. You looked at a teammate and you could see his nostrils twitching and sense his blood running. Somebody'd lift his fist up to say, "Let's go, this is the one!"

All these months and all these years.

I know I felt that. I know Jim Marshall did. I didn't know how well the man was going to play, but I knew one thing: He never wanted to play more in his life. His life was ballplaying, and this could be the summing-up of twenty years for him. He lifted his fist, nodded his head, and fixed his chinstrap. He was dying for the kickoff.

The Super Bowl gurus and television producers were going to make it a happening to surpass a decade of Super Bowls—and maybe thirty years of television. There were 100,421 people in the Rose Bowl, and they were all being stagecast. Everybody was going to be an actor. Where else but in California? The stadium attendants issued flashcards for a halftime show that would unite the two cultural phenomena of Twentieth Century America—Disneyland and pro football.

If you didn't have a card, maybe you had a black sock to announce your allegiance to Oakland.

A few hundred Viking fans came with their own emblems: purple jockstraps.

That may have been the ultimate phenomenon.

Even after it had started the good elves still seemed to be lining up with the Viking kicking teams, if not their brothers. For two months the Vikings were a football team that seemed directed by some psychic force bent on spreading a little justice to the people in the purple hardhats. It had healed their critical injuries in time, matched them against patsies when these were needed, emboldened them to their best against the best. Against L.A. a blocked kick had bounced into Bobby Bryant and become a 14-point play. And in the third minute of Super Bowl XI, Errol Mann popped a little field goal for the Oakland Raiders from the Viking 29.

The ball hit the upright and caromed off without harm.

In the 11th minute of Super Bowl XI, Ray Guy backed up to punt from the Oakland 19.

Fred McNeill: "As we saw them on film, they line up pretty tight. Charles Phillips was the end on their left side of their punt formation, so I lined up behind Windlan Hall of our team. Phillips had to come in tighter. When he got set I shifted five yards outside of him. He was set then, so he couldn't move. I got a good charge off the line, Phillips was too close to block me, and Windlan occupied Neil Colzie. That created an alley for me. I took four steps and dived. The timing was right, and I nicked the ball with my arm."

The ball flopped toward the Oakland goal line with the usual frantic posse in pursuit. McNeill covered it at the 3. The good elves trotted back to the Viking bench with Nate Allen, McNeill and the rest of the bunch. The auguries were still right for the Minnesota Vikings. Detroit, Milwaukee, Met Stadium, windchill or coastal breezes, it didn't matter. Dozens of purple jockstraps flapped in the stands. Big Philyaw stopped Foreman on the 2, but they had three downs left to punch over. Brent McClanahan smashed into the pile, lunging for the goal line and the one-touchdown lead that in Super Bowls past had usually shaped the action for the rest of the game.

Ron Yary: "Stu Voigt and I doubled Villapiano on the previous play, the one with Foreman. But the next play with McClanahan was such a quick hitter that I didn't go after Villapiano because there's no way the linebacker has the time to come in and make the tackle. So I helped Chuck Goodrum block on Philyaw. I can't believe Villapiano could make that tackle."

Phil Villapiano: "I wasn't going to get double-teamed again.

191

So I ducked Yary and Voigt both and shot into the backfield about the time the ball was being handed off. I didn't want them to score, but I wasn't thinking about a fumble. My helmet hit the ball. The ball came loose. I heard grunting and yelling."

Willie Hall recovered the ball for Oakland.

On the sidelines the elves turned to leave.

Snake Stabler entered the huddle, stared at Art Shell, John Vella, Dave Dalby and Gene Upshaw for a moment, and said, "Do it."

He didn't say "immediately." Pete Banaszak was stacked up twice, and now it was third and seven at the Oakland 6. For Kenny Stabler, it was a passing down. He had the studs and the thoroughbreds and the good steady glands to throw the ball anytime he wanted. The Vikings would look for that. Force an Oakland punt here and even Guy couldn't put it much past midfield. Tarkenton strapped on his helmet on the sideline and got ready. But Stabler called a run.

Jeff Siemon: "They called an off-tackle play with Clarence Davis carrying. He saw the inside congested and then bounced outside. In our eagerness to stop the off-tackle play, most of us got caught up in the inside. One of our guys came too far to the inside and I yelled and did everything but push him out of the way, but we lost leverage on the ball carrier. Shell, Upshaw and Dave Casper did some tremendous blocking for them. Jim Marshall and Alan Page had plugged up the inside; Wally and I got pinched off, Bryant was neutralized and there went Davis for 35 yards. I don't know if it was the turning point. I do know it established something that was never reversed after that."

The elves left the Viking bench because the football game was over.

If the Raiders could execute a basic running play like that from their own goal line and turn it into a 35-yard gain on raw force and technique, they could do it all day.

The Raiders saw that.

And so, perhaps, did the Vikings.

Errol Mann kicked the field goal for an Oakland lead, 3–0, to start the second quarter. They had gone 97 yards by running behind Shell and Upshaw and throwing to Casper. It was what they had intended to do, and nothing that wore purple was going to change that today. The next time they went 64 yards for a touchdown. In the process they introduced Fred Biletnikoff and all his gunky ointments. And the third time they went 35 after Colzie brought a punt back 25 yards. It was 16–0 and the Viking offense offered no real rebuttal. Tarkenton gimped around ineffectually. The deep passes he did throw well were dropped. Foreman ran with a kind of hopeless rage. He could not have played harder, or much better, but the Oakland defense shut down everything else and relatively soon it had Foreman under control.

Behind the overpowered Viking defensive front Jeff Siemon was playing his game of the season and one of the games of his life. Before the day was over he would make sixteen tackles and knock down a couple of Stabler's throws. He was expected to make tackles, of course, because the Vikings had structured their defense to make the middle linebacker a virtual rover (or wolfman) assigned to reduce the pressure on the Viking right side. Still, he played beyond the requirements of the strategy. It was one football player's response to the big-game demands of his calling, playing on familiar landscape again and confronting a crisis that gripped his team from the moment it failed to score on the goal line.

He had no illusions about a heroic figure role.

Jim Marshall might have been heroic, but he was struggling against Art Shell and nearly twenty years of attrition, and the remarkable old man just wasn't big enough. They blew him out. They did the same to Wally Hilgenberg and a lot of times to Alan Page and sometimes Jeff Siemon. You could add Mick Tingelhoff and the others when the Vikings were on offense.

In their mental blueprint of the ball game, the Vikings had pretty well planned on blotting out John Matuszak and Dave Rowe, and they fully expected a productive day's hammering on Phil Villapiano, the Raiders' left linebacker. But Matuszak and Rowe gave the Vikings nothing to exploit and Villapiano didn't make a mistake all afternoon. He did make seven tackles and forced a goal-line fumble. The Oakland defensive line didn't have to be all-pro. With Villapiano, Monte Johnson, Willie Hall and Ted Hendricks behind them, the Oakland defense achieved what nobody had all season. It had Tarkenton grabbagging for plays, groping for something that might work. In the Raider secondary Atkinson and Tatum took turns molesting the Viking receivers, legally for the most part. But they also threw forearms and a few fists masquerading as tackles, and the Vikings seemed grateful when they could get up.

Sammy White: "They were throwing clotheslines to the head all day. Just like they did all season. Some of those were pretty bad and should have been penalized. Tatum knocked my helmet off with one like that. The officials never call them, so we didn't yell about it, but that's something this league should stop."

George Atkinson: "It was hard to believe it when the Viking bench didn't say a word after I yelled at Foreman on a tackle."

Wally Hilgenberg: "He talked the whole game to Foreman. When you play pro football you figure you might get beaten by somebody's arm or foot or muscle or brains. You don't lose to his mouth. Whether you win or lose you don't have to run around like screaming gorillas to prove to the world you're a football player."

In the booths and sound trucks the television producers were swearing and groaning before the half was over. While the show might have been a rhapsody for Oakland fans, it was a 12-tone bust as theater.

There are certain kinds of athletic contests in which the destruction and interment of the weak can fascinate the viewer. The spectator is sometimes excited in the presence of crushing superiority. It gives him the feeling he is witnessing somebody or something historic—the best of this or the greatest of that. Joe Louis used to arouse that sensation in the 1930s and 1940s. The New York Yankees did the same thing—and for a couple of years the Chicago Bears and, of course, Notre Dame.

But there was a difference between the Oakland Raiders flattening some defenseless duck and, say, the Green Bay Packers of Lombardi doing it. With the Packers you didn't object to a certain amount of controlled slaughter. When it involved the Oakland Raiders vs. the Minnesota Vikings in Super Bowl XI, however, it looked a like a ripoff. Millions of people strolled to the biff during the timeouts shaking, among other things, their heads. The good old predictable Minnesota Vikings: Put them in the Super Bowl and watch them blow.

They didn't die on the sidelines. But in the heat and misery, some of them wanted to yell, "Jesus Christ, we're doing it again!"

Somebody read the halftime statistics on television during a break in the card show, and it reminded the older viewers of Roosevelt vs. Landon in 1936. The Raiders had 16 first downs, Minnesota 4. Oakland had 288 yards to 86. Oakland already had 166 yards on the ground to 27 for the Vikings, and they had run 48 plays to 22 for Minnesota. Instead of the teams going into the dressing rooms at halftime, somebody said, they should have gone to Appomattox or the deck of the battleship Missouri. The score, only 16–0 for Oakland, was fraudulent.

The Vikings listened to their coaching assistants for awhile and then to Bud Grant. He didn't have to remind them they had trailed badly or simply played badly in playoff games before, and rallied to win. They had played like sluggards for thirty minutes against the Redskins two years ago and wound up winning big. There was another game years before that, which Page, Marshall, Eller, Hilgenberg, Tingelhoff, Cox, Krause and some of the others remembered, when they came out brawling to beat the Rams after trailing by ten points.

But Page, Marshall, Eller, Hilgenberg, Tingelhoff, Cox and Krause were seven years younger then. This may have explained why they were now down, 16–0, to Shell, Upshaw, Davis, Stabler, Atkinson and the rest.

Grant's voice was under control, but it trembled slightly because the coach knew all about the embarrassment that lay ahead unless they turned the game around. But he didn't know any more than the electrician's wife from Sleepy Eye, Minnesota, in the 34th row why his football team looked so indisputably lousy and the Raiders looked like Caesar's army.

"We can lose this game," he said, "or we can make this one of the greatest victories in pro football. There's time to do it. They haven't got that many points."

Chuck Foreman didn't hear Grant. He was crying, he was pitched that high. Some of the old lions may not really have believed Chuck in the role of spiritual leader of the go-crazy crusade, but Foreman believed. He had tried to shove them, pull them and tough-talk them into a mood of eye-rolling zealotry, and when he got onto the field he had nearly run berserk. But it was 16–0 at halftime. The jivey month, all the talk and feisty attitudes had been twisted into a burlesque at which the whole country would jeer two hours from now—except for Chuck Foreman, whose eyes were moist, and his pals, whose eyes looked deadened and baffled.

The Vikings may have believed Bud Grant at that, even after the Raiders lifted their lead, 19–0, on another field goal in the third quarter. Tarkenton reorganized the Viking offense. He got a break when Hendricks ran into Neil Clabo on a punt, but he then passed to Voigt, Foreman, Rashad, Foreman again and then eight yards into the end zone to Sammy White. They had it up to 19–7 and, while the producers stared in rising joy, Tarkenton moved the Vikings toward the Oakland goal line once more to open the fourth quarter.

They reached the Raider 35 and stood second down with a yard to go. Despite all those suffocating statistics of the first half, the Vikings were 35 yards from turning a scenic disaster into an aurora borealis of television football.

Who would believe it?

Certainly not Monte Johnson of the Oakland Raiders linebackers.

On second down and a yard to go, Tarkenton called for

196

Chuck Foreman. It was not the least predictable call, but it probably was the best. Monte Johnson, however, had no intention of being predictable.

Ed White, Viking guard: "He lined up right behind John Matuszak. When he's in that position, I move around Ron Yary to block for the ball carrier. But this time Johnson took it inside and blitzed. He came straight through with nobody to stop him."

And Foreman lost two yards. On third and three from the Raider 37, Tarkenton dropped back to throw. The Mad Stork, Hendricks, blitzed from the outside and threatened to swallow Tarkenton. Struggling for balance, Francis turned and saw Foreman breaking toward the middle. He threw without strength in his haste to avoid dismemberment. Willie Hall timed his leap and intercepted.

The rest of it was a horror for the team that never had a gram of doubt about winning its first Super Bowl. The interception restored the Raiders' cavalier character, and they played the rest of the game in style: chippy, rude, elegant, brutal and unbeatable.

Their secondary behaved with the decorum of demolition derby drivers turned loose in a parking lot, but they surrendered nothing deep and they nearly buried anybody with the gall to catch anything close. When they needed something important they threw to Biletnikoff. He was not only a great receiver with moves and instincts but he was a walking gluepot. He carried enough adhesive on his hands and eyebrows to seal the Grand Canyon, and he never missed the ball.

The Raiders were a cornucopia of gifted, driven characters. They were Stabler's far underrated craftsmanship at quarterback. They were Shell and Upshaw dictating conditions on the line of scrimmage. They were Matzoh Ball, Kick-in-the-Head and Dr. Death. The labels were the emblems of a kind of chaotic and defiant brotherhood. They believed; they made their football team the expression of their hungers for the sun and their quirky creativity. Beside them the Vikings, for all their

December élan, were the portraits of cumbersome orthodoxy. They attended all their practices, they went to the right shows, they looked nice in public and they won an uncommon number of football games.

But they bombed in the Super Bowl.

Again.

When it was over Foreman disappeared from the reporters for a half hour to let his anger and his tears drain away. Grant stood up and called Oakland great, reminding those who were willing to keep a straight face that nobody had played in four Super Bowl games, nobody had made as much money in Super Bowl games—

"And nobody else," whispered a man from San Francisco, "has made two first downs rushing the whole game in three different Super Bowl games."

Grant was asked if all the arrangements for Super Bowl XI had met with his approval. "All," he said, "except one. They should have played the game on a Wednesday instead of Sunday."

A man asked Alan Page why Page's post-game summation was so brief.

"How many ways," Page asked, "can you spell ass-kicking?"

Didn't he think the Vikings might have tried something different?

"Yes," he said. "We should have stayed home."

From Jeff Siemon's journal

Monday, January 10 It was over and I wanted to answer all of the stupid questions as fast as I could and get out of that awful little locker room. The room was so small and there were so many reporters crammed into it that after I had gone and showered and come back, I had to stand and dry off five feet from my locker because some of the reporters were crammed in that, too.

I felt miserable physically. My hands and elbows were swollen, and it had been so hot that I was drained. I got through the postmortems and met my brother for a few minutes outside, then got on the team bus for the long ride to our hotel in Costa Mesa. You could reflect then. It was the whole thing all over again. The game seemed to have borrowed something from Dickens' "Christmas Carol": the Ghost of Super Bowls Past. I thought about all the others, but this was worse because we had paraded our eagerness and our goals in front of the whole country, and then we just got taken apart, as though we really couldn't compete with those people. With all the winning we've done in the last ten years, that was impossible to swallow. I don't really know why we played so badly.

Oakland, of course, was tremendous. It was one of the best teams I've played against. But we're so much better than we were in Pasadena, so much better.

I had doubts about the future, but that was for the future. This was still the day of the latest Super Bowl fiasco. I dreaded the team party in the hotel at night. I assumed a lot of guys would duck out, but they all showed up. They came with relatives, and there were hundreds of people, and the more I talked with them the more I remembered all the games we won.

I talked with Bud. He is an extraordinary guy, when you come to think of it. He talked about the defeat and about its place in our lives. He talked about all the positive sides to the season, and he seemed interested in my plans, my thoughts. We just talked ten minutes, man-to-man, and I don't know when I've been more impressed by anybody I've met in athletics. He ended smiling.

It wasn't long after that that a wonderful sense of peace engulfed me. I knew that in the midst of all this frustration, God had again sustained me. He allowed me to put the Super Bowl back into perspective—a vastly important game, yes, but by far not the most important thing in my life. I was discouraged, yes, but I was so anxious to see how God would use it for a positive purpose in my life.

One of Jeff's teammates, not quite as Christian, thought he could be just as positive if the Vikings won one of these things some day.

199

14

Mathematicians discount the theory that the Vikings cannot win the Super Bowl under any conditions, on any field and against any opponent.

The theory gained wide currency in the days immediately following Super Bowl XI and to this day it retains many stubborn adherents. Estimates of their strength vary widely, but a conservative guess might be 75 million—roughly the number who watched Super Bowl XI.

The mathematicians say no. They maintain that facts not now in evidence—whole new generations of data somewhere in the indistinct future—might be compatible with a Minnesota Viking victory in the Super Bowl.

They offer nothing specific. One theorized that the best hope for a Minnesota Viking Super Bowl championship lies in the potential return of the Ice Age.

"There's substantial evidence," he said, "that we are really living in an interlude between phases of the Ice Age and that the great glaciers will inevitably return, concealing most of the North American continent beneath layers of ice hundreds of feet thick.

"With time to prepare," he said, "civilization should be able to survive this vast entombment with some form of nuclear additive to keep society functioning underground. It follows that if life goes on in the next Ice Age, there will be football. If there is football, there will be a Super Bowl. If there is a Super Bowl in the Ice Age, the Minnesota Vikings have to be favored and one day might actually win."

He refused to cast that in the form of a flat prediction, pleading scientific restraint.

The history of the Super Bowl tends to support the scientists' conclusion that the Vikings thus far have not found the compatibility they need to win the big game. They are not compatible with the cities of New Orleans, Houston or Pasadena in January. To remove any doubt about New Orleans, they proved their incompatibility there twice. In New Orleans the first time they didn't like their hotel. In Houston there were sparrows in their shower room. In New Orleans the second time Howard Cosell showed up in their hotel the day before the game. In Pasadena they liked everything except Sunday. They have also shown themselves to feel awkward in the presence of the Kansas City Chiefs, Miami Dolphins, Pittsburgh Steelers and Oakland Raiders in January.

It is clear from this resume that the Vikings so far have functioned as disoriented waifs in the Super Bowl. The right environment obviously has eluded them. The Great Klondike Basin when the salmon are running has been suggested as a place more congenial to the Viking temperament.

The National Football League, for one, proceeded this fall on the premise that the Vikings actually are capable of winning the Super Bowl. The league office refused to honor the previously cited demands from the L.A. press to ban the Vikings from the playoffs, where they always eliminate the Rams, and from the Super Bowl, where the Viking presence has offended the artistic sensibilities of the California critics.

The league instead decided to continue the playoff system, which means the Vikings are almost certain to reach the postseason tournaments sometime in the next couple of years and probably eliminate the Rams again.

A lively mythology has already grown up around Viking futility in the Super Bowl. It demands some rebuttal from the truth. The Vikings have not been trampled in every Super Bowl. They lost one by only ten points. They have not been held to two first downs rushing in every Super Bowl, only in three of them. They have not lost to the Kansas City Chiefs in 85 Super Bowls (an impression widespread among television watchers from the number of times Cosell exhumes the game on Monday night).

They have, however, played terrible football in the Super Bowl—or at least it has been made to look terrible. The Minnesota Vikings, in the four Super Bowl games they have played in eight years, lost to Kansas City, 23–7; to Miami, 24–7; to Pittsburgh, 16–6; and to Oakland, 32–14. There is no analogous record of failure at the highest level of major league competition in recent history. The Brooklyn Dodgers spread their misery over a longer period. In contrast, the Vikings have compacted their defeats. It is theoretically possible for some slow-moving sweethearts to have spent a substantial part of their courtship in front of a television set watching the Vikings lose the Super Bowl.

Before you attack the question of whether this team can *ever* win the Super Bowl, you should try to discover why they have lost them all. The juiciest bone for the analysts is not that they have lost four out of four—which is not all that improbable for a good football team—but that they have lost so dreadfully. In three of their defeats they trailed by at least 16 points at halftime. In the other, the Pittsburgh game, they lagged by only two points at halftime but were mauled physically from the start.

Were they outgeneraled technically?

In Super Bowl IV in January 1970, the slim one week of preparation time between the conference title games and the Super Bowl probably left the Vikings less ready than Kansas City. The Chiefs presented novel defenses and an attack Coach

Hank Stram exuberantly described as the offense of the 1970s. Nothing so ambitious was required. So it actually became the offense of January 11, 1970, and it was adequate. Without a large file on the Chiefs, the Viking staff grubbed around and felt little comfort about its state of preparedness. The Viking defense, on the other hand, consisted chiefly of Alan Page, Carl Eller, Jim Marshall, and Gary Larsen, the best front four in football at the time. The Vikings lined up in a standard four-three defense on every play. They won their football games with better manpower, not complicated formations. Tactically, the Chiefs could have prepared for them between the national anthem and the kickoff. But the Chiefs won easily because Jan Stenerud kicked three long field goals in the first half, the offense of the 1970s produced two touchdowns and the Vikings, Joe Kapp and all, were duds.

Against Miami four years later the Vikings might have erred tactically by overhauling their offense to accommodate the Miami three-man line. But it wasn't the offense that lost the game. Larry Csonka and his herd scored two touchdowns in the opening minutes by caving in the Viking front and linebackers, and the crowd spent the rest of the game watching the blimp.

Against Pittsburgh the next year the defense didn't lose the game, the offense did—if you want to be parochial about it. If you want to be a Steeler about it, Pittsburgh devoured the Viking attack with L. C. Greenwood, Joe Greene, Dwight White and Ernie Holmes, Jack Lambert, Jack Ham, Mel Blount and anybody else you want to name. The game was close at the finish only theoretically. Franco Harris made over 140 yards, and the Vikings had to block a punt to score.

Against Oakland two years later the offense didn't lose the game and the defense didn't lose the game; the NFL did by scheduling the game on a Sunday.

It is almost impossible to imagine any wild combination of events that would have permitted the Vikings to beat Miami. The Dolphins may have been the best football team in pro history in the two years they won the Super Bowl in the 1970s.

The Vikings' loss to Pittsburgh was physical, deflating enough to convince some of the defeated players that sometimes survival is a legitimate end in itself.

Their only protest with Oakland was in trying to knot their ties after the game with Fred Biletnikoff's tar and jelly all over their hands.

They may have had a better team than Kansas City—but probably not.

The unremarkable truth their public has never been ready to consider is that the Vikings lost four Super Bowl games to superior teams. The world at large has no trouble with that conclusion. Certainly The Kansas City Chiefs, Miami Dolphins, Pittsburgh Steelers and Oakland Raiders don't. The Viking fans, however, like fans from Lapland to McMurdo Sound, surround their football team with a montage of victorious symbols and visions, like a child's scrapbook: mobs on the field, goalposts falling, triumphant faces glistening in sweat through the birdcages, white hats, indomitability, immortality—the Super Bowl.

Don't tell the Viking fan his football team shouldn't or can't win there.

And don't make him watch while his football team makes a jackass out of his white steed of hope.

What kind of justice, what kind of gratitude is that, he demands, for all his valiant support in front of the television screen?

The best Viking team, in the context of the times in which it played, never reached the Super Bowl. This was the Viking team of 1971, which lost in the first-round playoff to Dallas, the eventual Super Bowl champion. It was the only time in the last nine years that a National Football Conference team won the Super Bowl, and the only year when the NFC was clearly the dominant conference. The Viking defensive stars were in their competitive and physical prime, and the offense was sound and balanced.

Throwing out the Super Bowl's first two years, when the AFC

was a sacrificial offering to Lombardi's Packers, the old American Football League—now the AFC—plays better football than the NFC. It is a statement that is really beyond reasonable dispute. The best football teams in the NFL last year, for example, probably were, in order, Oakland, Pittsburgh, New England and Baltimore. The NFC offered the Minnesota Vikings and Los Angeles Rams, who played against each other twice last year without establishing much of anything except that the Rams don't seem to be able to win the NFC championship under two conditions: minus windchill (in Minnesota) and 75-degree weather (in Los Angeles, against Dallas, two years ago). They have not been tested in the Java rain forests or the Mongolian steppes.

The AFC's present superiority dodges easy explanation. It is really not a matter of style. If you want to argue that Oakland's roistering hearts and buccaneer camaraderie represent the AFC at its best, what about the Miami Dolphins under Shula a few years ago? The Pittsburgh Steelers are not the most suppressed spirits in football, but the whole orientation of the team, from the owner to the veteran players, has the old-league personality.

Critics have a tendency to lay down eternal truths on the evidence of last year's scoreboard. The Oakland Raiders, in the makeup of their team or the wily conduct of their management, aren't necessarily symbols or trailblazers. What they did was win the Super Bowl XI. If Oakland was pure AFC, from management to coach to players, the Pittsburgh Steelers the previous two years weren't. Nor were the Miami Dolphins before that, in the coaching department. Shula wins in any league.

Neither conference has any special dominance in the category of chaotic management, although the NFC, with Atlanta, New Orleans, Detroit and New York has a slight lead over the AFC, with its New York and Houston. It's probably true that the AFC has stronger and bolder management from top to bottom, leadership more likely to turn a loser into a winner faster. Oakland's Al Davis maintains the AFC arrived at its current superiority in the last big draft before the leagues merged, when the AFC had fewer teams, chose wisely and did not have to spread its talent as thinly as the NFC.

The coaching certainly isn't any different. Owners being the impetuous perfection seekers and glory chasers they are, the coaches move with the wind in both leagues and, like wandering pollen, settle on the most convenient sprout in either league. The result, or course, is crossbred coaching. Thus Shula goes from the NFL cidatel of Baltimore to the AFC sandbox of Miami and produces a Super Bowl champion. Joe Thomas, once strictly an NFL talent broker, leaves Minnesota to recruit a champion for Miami of the AFC. He wars with Shula and executive Joe Robbie in Miami and settles in Baltimore, where he turns an established and successful football team into a first-year franchise by tearing it up from top to bottom. Baltimore, now reconstituted as a typical AFC team, suddenly becomes a winner. And Thomas quits to join San Francisco of the NFC.

The AFC does have better quarterbacks in the aggregate (headed by Stabler, Bert Jones, Ken Anderson, Joe Ferguson and Terry Bradshaw). But the great running backs are evenly distributed (O. J. Simpson, Franco Harris and Otis Armstrong for the AFC, Chuck Foreman, Walter Payton and Lawrence McCutcheon for the NFC).

The difference, to the extent that it exists, may be largely in the management at that—the blunders that some make and others do not. The most dramatic illustration may be the Central Division of the National Football Conference, once the strongest in football. The Halas family, so distinguished in the formative years of football, allowed the Chicago Bears to deteriorate into squabbling nonentities on the field. They are being restored under the orchestration of Jim Finks. The Detroit Lions are still erratic administratively. The Green Bay Packers, with a couple thousand stockholders, sank to ineptness when Lombardi left. His departure threw the organization back into chancy thrashings of democracy-at-work.

Only the Vikings in the Central Division have stayed in their orbit through all this. They absorbed a major management upheaval when Finks quit in the spinoff of a power shift on the board of directors from Bernie Ridder, a St. Paul newspaper publisher, to Max Winter, a Minneapolis sports promoter and entertainment figure. But the fixed axis for the Vikings for ten years has not been its management, or even some of its great stars, but the head coach, Grant.

Their stability is due to Grant's understated skills in achieving harmony and a team-oriented atmosphere around such individualists as Tarkenton, Page, Yary, Siemon, Foreman and Eller. With it the Vikings outdistanced all rivals in the Central Division and all but Dallas and Los Angeles in the conference generally. If much of the time they played like automatons, Grant did not object. It meant consistency. And consistency meant winning. And winning meant you reached the playoffs. Where other teams might have superior personnel in a given year or might play better much of the time, Grant's teams played acceptably well almost *all* of the time. This meant that now and then they might win a playoff game they shouldn't have won—especially if they played the game in Metropolitan Stadium in December against the Rams.

One reason the Minnesota Vikings lost four Super Bowl games is that at least once or twice they shouldn't have been there. That is, they beat a better team to get there. The Rams of 1976 probably were a better football team than the Vikings. They blew their chances to make the Super Bowl not on officials' lousy calls, as the Rams organization howled, but on the timidity of their coaching staff in going for a field goal from the three-inch line in the first quarter—which, in turn, had something to do with the Rams' prior failures on the Minnesota goal line.

But none of this explains why the Vikings look so irredeemably awful in the Super Bowl.

The temptation is to look for fall guys; and the most visible fall guy on a team that loses championship games is the quarterback. Against a truly great team, the argument goes, Francis

Tarkenton's cunning and runabout quarterbacking can't win. This argument runs into trouble right away with its characterization of Tarkenton's style. He just doesn't run around much any more. And while he might not have thrown very far against Oakland, the Raiders' defense rarely can be attacked that way. He had to throw deep against Detroit and others, and he did. The accusation that Tarkenton can't win the big one belongs with the flying saucers and the abominable snowmen. It is an argument made of air. The same kind of charge used to be made against Tom Landry as coach of the Cowboys, and it wasn't much different for Al McGuire of the Marquette basketball teams.

And it's not the age of some of the Vikings' important players or the lack of heft in their defensive line (it went into the Super Bowl with an average weight not much greater than that of some of the bigger metropolitan high school teams) that offers clues to their unsightly pratfalls in the Super Bowl. They weren't too old or too light to win eleven games in the 1976 regular season—including an emphatic victory over the Pittsburgh Steelers.

What is it about the Super Bowl, then, that seems to unhinge this team?

Ed White might not be so far from the truth. The post-Pasadena ridicule infuriated him, but it also stirred him to an examination.

White is the 270-pound all-pro guard who has played in all four Super Bowls. He is one of the most powerful men in American athletics and a highly motivated competitor. Away from the caveman-in-ermine environment of the game, he is a thoughtful, even tender person, a youth counselor and a landscape painter.

He says he dies a little in playing in the Super Bowl. It has nothing to do with resolve or the quality of the competition or the bigger-than-us-humans scope of the game.

"I never like to talk about how I as a ball player react to the week of the Super Bowl," he said, "because it sounds like the lamest kind of alibi if you lose, and somebody always tells you, 'well, it's the same for both teams.'

"That's the point that bothers me. I don't think it's necessarily the same for both teams.

"We're pretty much a programmed football team. I don't think that's bad. The coach has eliminated just about all the extraneous stuff so that when we go to training camp we start a week after the other teams. When we practice during the season we get to the stadium a little before noon and we get out of there by 4:30. When we play a game on the road we fly out of Minnesota at the last possible hour that will satisfy the league rules. When we get in we have a team dinner, have a couple of hours off, have a meeting and a snack, go to bed, get up, have breakfast, get taped, go to the park an hour before the game, play, get out of there and go home.

"In other words, you get your football in concentrated form under Grant. The ball players aren't falling over each other all day, hanging around hotel lobbies or hanging around the dressing room for a half hour waiting for somebody to poke his head in the door and say 'come on, let's go.'

"When it's football under Grant, it's football and nothing else. When it isn't football, get out of there and go home or wherever you go.

"The schedule and the routine almost never vary. Same times, same things. You don't get bored with it because you don't have a feeling of struggling with time and monotony. Also, they pay pretty well—so where do you get off being bored? It's Grant's way of protecting against staleness, making everything move on schedule and preventing football from becoming a sort of hovering thing that occupies you even when it can't command your attention.

"And it works.

"The team is usually pretty sharp the last month of the year when a lot of other teams are hanging on or drifting, already thinking about Hawaii.

"Then we go to the Super Bowl.

209

"It means a week in a hotel. It means two or three press conferences during the week, running around from hotel to practice field. It means you're going to a couple of parties during the week because there's nothing else to do with your time. They can't give you any more football than you usually play during the week, so you do a lot of cardplaying in your room or sitting around and calling home. And then you get a night with the wife on Friday and more contrived team meetings and a lot more cardplaying. You look around for diversions.

"Some of the more social creatures on the team come in contact with really beautiful diversions.

"So the fan might say, 'What the hell, I don't see that it's such a great hardship for guys hauling down 50 grand to 300 grand for one football game a week.'

"It isn't any hardship at all. But it is a helluva change. Without trying to make any self-serving excuse for how we've played in the Super Bowl, I'm just saying the change might affect us more than it does a team with a looser weekly routine during the season, where the programming hasn't been as close.

"I don't know if Grant would buy that kind of analysis. I think he's tried to adjust the team each time in a little different way to what it has to contend with, and I wouldn't second-guess it. Theories are easy—and meaningless. I wish I didn't have to try to explain, but when a thousand people ask you, and it's the first question they ask, you can't just stand there and stare like it's a stupid question."

Bud Grant does not consider it a stupid question. Why have his four National Football Conference flagships capsized so abjectly in the Super Bowl?

First, he doesn't believe there are any convincing explanations; second, he doesn't believe the team has played that badly.

Grant never mounts oratorical counterattacks against authors, commentators or fans who take offense at his football team's performance in the Super Bowl.

"Wiseguys and critics," he said, "or just plain teed-off fans aren't going to listen very seriously to the kind of explanation

I've got. And I'm not going to cry about that. It's part of losing the Super Bowl—or losing it four times, if you want to go into history.

"I don't look at the games that way—I mean historically, or as part of some overall pattern or scheme. Why we lost to Kansas City may be entirely different from why we lost to Miami, and I'm sure it was. So each game has to be looked at for what it has to tell you.

"If I said now that in at least one or two of those games there were officials' decisions or a series of decisions that were just as important as any plays made, that sounds like the thinnest alibi in the world, and nobody will listen. That it happens to be true is just not relevant. If I said in one of the games, the one with Pittsburgh, it was a standoff most of the time, not many people are going to remember that or will be willing to consider it.

"So we hear a dozen explanations and theories because the record seems to demand them. But it's just a lot of talk, isn't it? If millions of people think the Vikings are a bunch of wilting flowers in the Super Bowl, talk isn't going to change their minds.

"You know, nobody thinks of Oakland that way now. Oakland went year in and year out losing in the AFC playoffs. They also lost the only other Super Bowl game they played in, to the Packers back in the mid 1960s. So I'm sure the Oakland press and the grandstands were full of theories every year about why Oakland lost the big game.

"The rest of the country didn't think much about it because Oakland didn't show up in the Super Bowl all those years. But they did last year, and won, and now nobody is ever going to hear those stories again. But nobody ever did get an answer to why Oakland lost that streak of playoff games. The same way, I'm sure Chuck Knox can't tell you why the Rams have lost three NFC championship games in four years. When we've lost, it's been in the Super Bowl, with 75 million looking at the game. So our losses go into the public domain.

"Nothing that happened in Pasadena can change the things

we accomplished during the seasons. Almost everything we did, the trade for Rashad, the draft choices of Sammy White and a few others, the trades for Nate Allen, Windlan Hall and Sammy Johnson, avoiding serious injuries, winning the big games—all of those were sevens on the dice. And then it ran out. We threw craps. The Super Bowl turns the season into heaven or hell. It's glory or junk for two teams in football. Not for the others. They were judged by how many games they won, how they were at the finish, the crowds, all those normal things that decide whether you're successful or unsuccessful. In the Super Bowl you put the farm on the table and throw the dice and, as far as the country or even the shrewd guys are concerned, you're either the golden boys or the dogs.

"And I wouldn't change it. I really wouldn't be very surprised if the Vikings win the Super Bowl pretty soon. Even if they don't, I still wouldn't change the system.

"People ask me if I felt any personal chagrin late in the Oakland game, seeing we were losing another Super Bowl game. I did feel something. I looked down the bench one time and saw all the veterans who made this a great football team and I felt for them. It would be something to take away with you, winning the Super Bowl game. I never questioned that. But they weren't going to do it. Our fans have one coming, and I don't question that, either. It would be a tremendous trophy for them, and for the people who own the team.

"The coach doesn't really stew about embarrassing losses while he's coaching a game, especially if he knows the team he's coaching is a good one and has given him much all those years."

He still, after all, must coach. In the final moments of Super Bowl XI, when the crowd behind the Viking bench was venting its raspy judgment—and some in it wore purple eyeshades—Grant clasped Roy Winston by the arm and asked him if he wanted to finish out the game at linebacker. This was Moony, in his fifteenth season and probably headed for retirement, who took one of Grant's spirals in the snoot during a practice session but clowned about it later.

212

"Sure," he said. "Playing is what this is all about, isn't it?" So he ran into the ball game. And, like a rookie on opening day, Winston barged in to make a tackle. The game over, he thanked the coach.

Some day it would be nice to beam at the sight of a championship ring on his finger when the old clan gathers in some foggy bar on alumni day in the years to come.

But fifteen years of football have filled his head with enough memories, his jeans with enough coin and his body with enough scar tissue to compensate for the empty pedestal in his trophy cabinet.

Pedestals don't mean much alongside Hilgenberg's cackle, Tarkenton's rolling a football on his hands and knees in the locker room or Yary's shaving in full uniform.

Moony had a suggestion as the last of the Vikings' corps left the Rose Bowl.

"Bud," he said, "maybe they really ought to schedule this damned thing on Wednesday."